Everybody's Entitled To MY Opinion

BYRON F. DEMING

Everybody's Entitled to MY Opinion © 1990 by Byron F. Deming.

Cover Design • Pam McCarthy

Cover Production • Right Angle Productions

Book Design • Graphic Masters

Typesetting • GraphicMasters

Editor • Lynn McGinnis

Printers • McNaughton & Gunn

Library of Congress No. 90-84952

ISBN: 0-9627937-0-1

Printed in the U.S.A.

Published by:
Byron Mangement Company
P.O. Box 1591
Rocklin, CA 95677

DEDICATION

This book is dedicated to Senator Barry Goldwater who wrote *Conscience of a Conservative* unfortunately about 25 years before its time.

I also dedicate this book to my fellow couch potatoes and yellbirds who are very vocal on all issues but just sit around doing nothing but yelling "why don't **THEY** do something about it?"

And most of all I dedicate this book to my wife, Cynthia, and my daughters, Pam & Connie, who have tolerated (sometimes reluctantly) my spouting off my opinions on all subjects for many years.

P.S. Unfortunately my wife Cynthia, who was my patient sounding board, died September 17, 1990 before she could see this book in print.

TABLE OF CONTENTS

This book is intended as light reading for heavy thinkers. Opinions rule the world but only if they are known in the right places. Does yours count?

The IRS (unqualified self appointed business managers of our entire economy) should and can be reduced to merely collecting money to run the government.

What used to be a sport is now a combination of sumo wrestlers, computer experts, pugilistic giant multimillionaires, and an army of officials and cameramen. The rules committee has sadly mistaken rule changes for progress — a common malady.

Don't concentrate on arresting drug dealers, arrest drug users who don't carry Ouzi machine guns. It can be made to work.

Prison sentences should be in three parts — time served, further education requirement and public service time. It could be done at no additional cost to taxpayers.

Lawyers should be penalized for their failures instead of being rewarded for their inefficiency, but lawyers set the rules for lawyers.

How much do you know about your doctor's record? And wouldn't it be great to have the medical history of your entire life on a floppy disk?

You voted for the rascals who can't stop spending — what are YOU going to do about it? It takes all the taxes collected west of the Mississippi to pay the interest on the debt.

INTRODUCTION

Opinions are not to be looked upon lightly because they are the force that rules the world. Opinions are not to be confused with facts, knowledge or logic because those, in most cases are completely separate subjects. We vote (or not vote) based on our opinions. Countries start wars based on their collective opinions that they can win the war and will prosper one way or another, by ego gratification, material goods or something else. You get your opinions from many sources such as your church, parents, newspapers, books, governments, neighbors, friends, political parties, fortune cookies, palm readers, television, and personal experiences. It makes no difference where you got your opinions, they rule your actions and your life. They consciously or subconsciously form predictions which ultimately guide our lives. It is well known that Hitler's opinions were heavily influenced by stargazers and fortune tellers. Almost all decisions made in this world have been based on somebody's opinions so don't look upon them lightly.

This book is intended to be light reading for heavy thinkers and is an exercise in creative thinking. It is written on a subject on which I am the undisputed worldwide authority — my own opinions. In spite of its being so authoritative, it required a tremendous amount of thought and practically no research in its preparation. Many of the thoughts expressed herein venture into unexplored territory and little is known about them due to lack of experience. No specific amount of knowledge, experience or intelligence is required to form an opinion, however all three of these ingredients are required to refine the opinion plus have the guts to say to yourself, "I was wrong," and then change the opinion. Unfortunately, many of us lack the guts and intellect to distinguish between "I believe" and "I know" or "it is" from "it might be." Forgive me for what I am about to do in this book.

If you really want to get to know someone well, you must get to know their opinions on many subjects. I wrote this book hoping it might become a prototype for all politicians aspiring for high political office. Senator Goldwater had the courage to expose himself with his book *Conscience of a Conservative,* and I feel all political candidates should do likewise. I wouldn't trust a candidate who refused to take his hair down on many controversial subjects.

Before we get started we must clarify and lay down the ground rules. Webster's Third New International Dictionary devotes the major portion of a large page trying to define "opinion" but it all boils down to this first definition:

Opinion — a view, judgment or appraisal formed in the mind about a particular matter or particular matters.

Notice it doesn't say anything about being an expert or even being knowledgeable on the subject or doing any research. Our opinions are formed subconsciously whether we work at them or not, and they are based upon our personal experiences (or the experiences of others as they are related to us), what we have read, heard or seen in person, seen on television, and sometimes just a lot of thought and raw emotions. How well we remember the details of what we heard or where we heard it is irrelevant for the opinion has been formed on the impressions retained, be they right or wrong. They are what influence our actions. This is what makes propaganda and advertising so successful. It's what you remember that counts and not where you heard it. You will remember the opinion long after you have forgotten the facts you used to form that opinion. Opinions may be changed at any time, may be reinforced with more data or hearsay, diminished or even forgotten over a period of time. Usually, after opinions are formed we are too lazy and opinionated to research the subject with an open mind because new facts may require us to change our opinions, which is often quite painful and embarrassing. Unfortunately we have a subconscious tendency to accept data that support opinions already formed and conveniently ignore those facts that don't support our opinion. How often have you heard the expression, "Don't give me the facts — I've already made up my mind"? You needn't laugh at how my opinions are formed because you are no different — yours are formed the same way even though our conclusions may differ based on the same facts.

If, at any time, you become bored or I hit a real raw nerve in any chapter, just stay calm and proceed to the next chapter, because there is no continuity of thought between chapters and each has its own plot so you won't have missed much if you skip around.

I have an overall opinion that most things in this world are (maybe deliberately) made too complex. If our laws were very simple, we wouldn't need so many lawyers. I don't subscribe to the philosophy that it must be complicated to be good. Therefore simplicity has invaded my opinions on almost every subject.

I realize there is a very tiny audience for a book of this nature because the world is made up mostly of people who like to spout off and there are relatively few people who want to listen. The ratio of talkers and complainers to listeners and doers is completely out of balance.

Several years ago the San Francisco Golden Gate Bridge Authority made a very substantial reduction in their operating expenses which should serve as a lesson to us all. The improvement cost absolutely nothing to implement and was so obvious it should have been designed into the bridge at the outset and incorporated into the operation of the bridge fifty years earlier. This very simple improvement consisted of closing all the northbound toll booths and doubling the toll charge for the southbound traffic. It costs twice the normal toll charge to enter the city but leaving it is free. It appears they have a rather unfriendly "get out of town for free" attitude. Since the southbound traffic is equal to the northbound traffic, not a penny of revenue was lost, except for those cheaters who bypass the bridge on their southbound trip and drive from Sausalito through San Rafael, through Ignacio, Novato, Vallejo, Benecia, across the Carquinez Bridge (in the free direction) through Rodeo, Hercules, Pinole, Richmond, Berkeley, Oakland, Hayward, San Mateo, Fremont, Mt. View, Sunnyvale, Palo Alto, San Carlos, Burlingame, San Bruno, South San Francisco and eventually to San Francisco. So forget it. There are some short cuts to this toll-dodging route, but they involve other toll bridges too. The cost of trying to cheat the system comes high. The intelligence of those who have tried this once is questionable, and those who tried it twice should be looked upon as dangerous to society. Considering the time involved, the car expense and jangled nerves involved with this alternate route makes the bridge and its toll charge a real bargain. This change of operating procedure resulted in a saving of 50% for the number of employees and all their associated expenses and benefits. Had this idea surfaced during the design of the bridge, additional money could have been saved by building half as many toll booths and gates. A second gigantic benefit was realized at the same time by this new operating procedure. Toll booths are a bottleneck to the flow of traffic, and there is now only one bottleneck where formerly there were two bottlenecks.

I once worked with a group of people who had a slogan they called "KISS," which is an acronym for Keep It Simple, Stupid. Had this philosophy been incorporated in the bridge fifty years ago many millions of dollars would have been saved and millions of commuters would have been spared hours of traffic bottlenecks on their trips home across the bridge and possibly a few black eyes.

In keeping with the KISS philosophy, I kept this a very short book by avoiding the temptation to elaborate on the obvious. "Etc." has been used generously throughout to avoid needless expansion of an idea in infinite detail. I'll give you the salient points and let you do the elaborating in your own mind.

This is a complicated world, so naturally we have been programmed to expect complicated solutions to our problems. When I was in college, my roommate and I were faced with a long final examination in Physics 1A containing far too many problems to be solved in the allotted time period. One of the problems described a situation where a man and his son had a pole that was 10 feet long and weighed 5 pounds resting on their shoulders and a bucket of water that weighed 10 pounds. The problem: "How can it be arranged so that the man carries twice as much weight as his son?" Those of us who have been programmed to antici-pate the complicated saw this problem as a leverage problem in physics and performed much time-consuming mathematics to find a solution, whereas my roommate saw this as a simple prob-lem in logic and wrote "Let the man carry the 10 pound bucket of water and let his son carry the 5 pound pole," and then he proceeded on to the next problem.

With this approach in mind, let us proceed with our search for the simple but not always the obvious. Unfortunately, ev-erything can't be as easy as the bridge example and the man and his water problem, but we should thoroughly explore the sim-plistic approaches before allowing things to get complicated.

In the interest of fairness to the reader, this book is an accu-mulation of ideas and opinions gathered in my mind over many years, and unfortunately some of the facts stated here are from memory. Memory was my worst subject in school (I flunked it), consequently many facts presented here should be given an ac-curacy factor of about plus or minus 10%, which doesn't signifi-cantly detract from the basic ideas. These ideas and opinions have not been lying around completely dormant over the years, for they have been aired out on many occasions (on my family and bored friends) and consequently updated many times. Now I feel they have reached a point of refinement where they are ready to be shared with the whole world.

Don't mistake this book as a case of "pick a subject and choose a side" just for the sake of a good argument for I have already picked my side, formed my opinions and am ready to defend them strongly to the bitter end (unless I'm convinced otherwise, at which time I'll sulk and remain very quiet for a while and then sheepishly change my opinion). You won't find many facts in the following text, for this is not a reference manual. It merely represents an attitude.

Our world is full of problems and injustices that need our attention, and they will remain problems unless you and I "get off our complacency" and make a vigorous effort to solve them. Simply sitting around wringing our hands and stewing will only give us ulcers, so let's try to make this a better world. In most cases, in the following chapters, I have attempted to offer a possible solution to the problem. You may have a better solution — but do something.

Some of this is tongue-in-cheek — it's up you to guess which parts.

Chapter 1

INCOME TAXES

Here is a subject that is near and dear to my wallet, my sense of fair play and also a subject that causes the proponents of the KISS philosophy to vomit.

WE have a huge financial problem — WE, not they. We means everybody in the United States. The problem, simply defined, is that our government's income is less than its expenditures. And the solution to this unbalanced situation, very simply stated, is we must spend less or take in more taxes. There is another alternative used by other nations, and that is to borrow money and then announce they can't or won't pay it back. This scheme sounds unethical and dishonest to me. Only a fool would loan money to a government with this policy. This is no different than our own congress who has borrowed over three trillion dollars and has absolutely no intentions of ever paying it back (except with more borrowed money). Our borrowing has reached a point where it requires all the taxes collected west of the Mississippi River to pay the interest on our national debt. Still another idea which should be quickly discarded is go to war with Germany and Japan again and let them win this time so that we can dismantle our Department of Defense and save about a half a trillion dollars each year. Let's quickly bury these ideas before some idiot politician takes them seriously. Our politicians have proven over the past fifty years that they either don't understand our financial problem or they are purposely ignoring it because they can't overcome the urge to spend money. The sad part of this spending frenzy is that the politicians feel they must spend money favoring special interest groups in order to continuously get reelected, and worse yet, they are right, since 99% of all incumbents are reelected (FACT). After a little thought, it is obvious that they are the smart ones and we (the voters) are the dummies. It appears our best hope for a solution is to reduce government expenditures by streamlining our subsidy programs and our bureaucracies.

Let's analyze our income tax system. The IRS tax code has violated one of the most fundamental principles of good financial management which is to separate accounts receivable from accounts payable. Taxes must be separated from subsidies. Our current income tax system has divided all taxpayers into special interest groups through special interest deductions, which are really hidden subsidies being paid by all the other special interest groups. This problem will never go away until WE start acting like a single group of taxpayers by eliminating all these special interest group subsidies.

If everybody is subsidized, and we all are to some extent on the IRS 1040 form, the end result is that nobody is subsidized and nothing has been accomplished except a lot of costly paperwork has been generated and we have burdened ourselves with unproductive work dictated to us by congress and its bureaucrats.

All tax deductions are subsidies because if one group doesn't pay its fare share of the government's operating expense it means that others are paying more than their share. As an example let's use a ride club of five workers working a five day week with total transportation expenses of $20.00 per week. Each contributes $4.00 per week to the expense kitty. Rider number one receives a job promotion which entitles him to a very convenient supervisor's parking space in the company parking lot. It is decided that he will no longer be required to contribute to the expense kitty. The other four riders must pay an additional $1.00 per week to cover the expenses. At a later date the ride club is increased to six riders. When it is discovered the new member of the club is newly married, has just graduated from school and has a pregnant wife, it is decided to let him ride free. The chart below summarizes this subsidy program:

Rider's Weekly Transportation Expense Contribution.

Rider Number	#1	#2	#3	#4	#5	#6	Total
Original Club	$4	$4	$4	$4	$4		$20
New Supervisor		$5	$5	$5	$5		$20
Additional Rider		$4	$4	$4	$4	$4	$20
Subsidized Rider		$5	$5	$5	$5		$20

The end result is the total weekly expense did not change, but four riders are now paying the transportation expenses of six riders because riders #1 and #6 are being subsidized and aren't paying their fair share. Is this any different than our current income tax 1040 form with its many subsidies?

Who should pay taxes? The simple answer is everyone who benefits from living or doing business in the United States. Taxes are a necessary evil at best except in Kuwait, the Principality of Monaco and maybe a few other nations with outside incomes, but their solution won't work here. Recognizing that we must live with this evil, let's make it as painless as we can. Our income tax system has degenerated over the years to a real "Rube Goldberg" scheme. For those unfortunate few who are not familiar with "Rube" (notice that I am on a first name basis with him) let Mr. Webster explain:

> Rube Goldberg — a cartoonist known for comic drawings of ridiculously complicated mechanical contrivances: accomplishing by extremely complex roundabout means what actually or seemingly could be done simply, crowded with a Rube Goldberg phantasmagoria of furnaces, grinders, tanks, mixers and countless unrecognizable contraptions.

Rube died on December 7, 1970, so the IRS and our lawmakers must struggle on without him, wallowing in their own ineptness. Rube would be proud of our income tax system whereby we accumulate large volumes of records, add up all the money we received during the year, total it, subtract a bunch of nonsensical totals (subsidies), multiply by some meaningless numbers and then go back and average that result with a few previous years' mathematical gyrations, pay the government and then stand by for an argument with the very guys who made up and interpret the rules of their game. Numerous tests have proven that a question to the IRS results in a wrong answer over 40% of the time, which would be a failing grade in any educational institution. We would all question a huge corporation that contracted an accounting firm composed of all academic failures to handle their financial affairs. Yet that's what we appear to have done with the IRS. It makes our own intelligence appear questionable.

This income tax battleground is no place for the light hearted or those with a weak stomach, so we bring in professional gladiators called tax accountants and tax lawyers. There are rules to this game like any other sport, but the big difference is that it is your livelihood they are enjoying kicking around and not a ball. The real irony of this ridiculous situation is that *you* are directly or indirectly paying the salaries of the tax accountants, tax lawyers, and bureaucrats who enjoy playing this game.

After all of the above arithmetic machinations, the result is that the taxes you paid amounted to X% of your total income. You can determine your net tax percentage by simply dividing the taxes you paid by your total income. You will find that most of your friends paid about the same rate if they played the income tax game as well as you. It appears this would be a good time to requote an excerpt from Webster's definition of Rube Goldberg "*what actually or seemingly could be done simply .*"

Think of a number between one and ten. Now add your age to it. Multiply this result by 2 and then add 3986. Divide by two and then subtract the year you were born minus twice the number you started with and then divide the final answer by 2. Voila! We now have your age. This kind of stuff is fun for kids, but taxes are serious business not to be taken lightly like a child's puzzle. If you want a lot of gamesmanship, fine, but if you only want to know my age just ask me and knock off the childish Hokey Pokey. There is a time and place for games and income tax preparation is not the place for games. If you tried this mathematical exercise you will find, like your 1040 tax form, it doesn't come out right.

How much does all this bureaucratic nonsense and gamesmanship really cost us in terms of dollars, mental anguish, lost time, frustration and worst of all a loss of competitive edge for our industry in the world marketplace? Nobody really knows, and if they do, it is one of the best kept secrets in the government. What is the total taxes not paid because of the deductions (subsidies) for interest payments, expense accounts, company cars, entertainment, etc., etc., etc.? We have become a nation of bureaucrats, bookkeepers, lawyers, accountants and cheaters in order to survive. It has finally come to the point where pocket computers are now for rent for $39 per month for the sole purpose of keeping records of expenses just to satisfy the IRS. A small tape is taken out of the computer monthly and mailed to the parent firm where your taxes are computed and records are maintained for seven years. Wouldn't it be nice if all that money and effort could be devoted to something constructive like raising the GNP (Gross National Product) or just having fun? How much money are we really talking about if everyone was forced to carry one of these bookkeeping machines? Eighty million taxpayers times $39 per month, times twelve months per year is WOW ($37,440,000,000 per year). As the late Senator Everett Dirksen used to say "a billion here and a billion there and pretty soon we're talking about some real money."

Now if I'm wrong and the ultimate purpose of all this excessively complicated system is to keep tax accountants, tax lawyers and bureaucrats employed at the expense of the tax-paying public, then let's do it up right and file a 1040 form on the 15th of every month instead of just April 15th. To make things even more complicated, let's revise the tax code every three months to prevent anybody from becoming too familiar with it.

And then there is the capital gains tax which is a completely unjustified farce. We are being taxed on something that doesn't exist. Let's call it by its real name "Inflation Tax." I remember the first house we ever bought, which was in 1951. That new house cost us $9,000, which was about ten times the price of a new car. Our next house cost us a hell of a lot more money but still about ten times the price of a new car. Thirty years after we bought our first house we bought another house which cost us $150,000 and, yes, you guessed it, it was about ten times the price of a new car. This same comparison can be made to the price of clothes, food, rent, etc. The results will be about the same. The only thing that has happened over the years is that the value of the dollar went down so there was no capital gains at all, but there was a substantial loss in the value of the dollar. It would be very difficult to find any justification or basis for a tax here, and it makes one wonder what the politicians and bureaucrats were thinking about when this tax was instituted. Did they know what they were doing and figured the taxpaying public is so dumb and helpless it won't question anything? From now on let's be honest and refer to that tax as INFLATION TAX, for that's what it really is.

After the kids are through school and have left home, the big family home is no longer a necessity and it is time to start getting the living expenses in line for retirement. Selling the big house in order to buy a less expensive house can come as a real surprise because this is when you find out that the government owns a substantial share of your current house. The government's share is called capital gains. This applies to all the houses you have ever owned previously if you have deferred your capital gains tax each time you bought a more expensive new home. Hope you have kept good records of purchase prices, improvements, selling expenses, sales price, etc., because there is no statute of limitations on federal taxes. The IRS does have a small humanitarian streak, but even that is stupidly administered. After you have reached a certain age, you are permitted to sell your home and have a one time forgiveness tax benefit of $125,000 *if* you and your spouse are both over 55 years of age, *if* you have lived in the house over three years, *if* blah, blah, blah, blah. Why all the ifs? If it's a good idea to stop punishing people for growing old, retiring and replacing the no longer needed large house with a smaller one, then give them the tax break and forget all the hoops they have to jump through to get the tax break. Furthermore, if a $125,000 tax break was a good idea several years ago, then with inflation (decreased value of the dollar) it should be about $250,000 today, which assumes a modest rate of inflation of about 5% per year. Here again inflation works for the government but does not apply when it is in favor of the taxpayer. That term "forgiveness" is a fascinating term. It implies a wrong has been committed. If there is any forgiving to be done, it should come from the taxpayer to the government for having levied their illegal INFLATION TAX on us for all these years. The part that really hurts most is that this all occurs at the time of retirement when almost everybody's income decreases and they can least afford additional taxes.

Guess there's no need to belabor the point further. I think we agree things could be better than they are now if everybody (including politicians and bureaucrats) would remember THE ONLY JUSTIFICATION FOR COLLECTING TAXES IS TO RAISE MONEY TO OPERATE THE GOVERNMENT. Taxes should not be used to punish people, control the economy by forcing consumer spending into government designated channels, encourage or discourage spending (i.e. increasing your taxes if you save money and decreasing your taxes if you borrow money), or to make taxpayers subservient to the government.

We pretend we have a free enterprise economy, but this is definitely not true according to *Webster's Third New International Dictionary*:

> free enterprise n 1: an economic system in which primary reliance is placed upon private business operating in competitive markets to satisfy customer demands and to maintain equilibrium in the national economy in which government action in this respect is restricted to protecting the rights of individuals rather than acting as a directing force.

Do we have a free enterprise economic system or does the IRS qualify as a governmental directing economic force?

Criticism is meaningless without a suggested improvement. Here's how it should be done! Take a deep breath to clear your mind of the old system so you can be totally objective from here on. Remember, the ONLY justification for income taxes is to raise revenue to operate the government.

First we will do away with complicated income taxes as we know them today and replace them with different simple taxes. The income tax for wage earners would be replaced with a payroll tax. As you will recall from our previous discussion, we can arrive at our current amount of tax very simply by using a net tax percentage without going through all the arithmetic and record keeping required today. By way of illustration, let us assume that General Motors has a $100,000,000 monthly payroll at one of its divisions and further assume that the net tax percentage rate has been established at 10%. General Motors would pay its employees $90,000,000 and mail a single check to the Treasury Department for $10,000,000 and that's the end of it. There are no tax deductions under this system, therefore there is no need to fill out and file any of the 342 IRS tax forms on April 15th. Furthermore there is no need for GM to even list the names of the employees, just the bucks that were earned in salaries, wages and bonuses. The IRS would receive one check from each employer, not millions of checks from the millions of employees. The IRS would only have one account to audit at a later date: GM's payroll department. That pretty much takes care of wage earners.

Next we will tax retail sales. This is a national *retail* sales tax and no more complicated than sales tax in most states now. Let's assume a national sales tax percentage rate of 5%. For example, when a merchant makes retail sales amounting to $100,000 he charges his customers $105,000 and sends the $5,000 difference to the Treasury Department, and his taxes have been paid.

What could be more simple? No merchant has ever gone broke collecting sales taxes for the government. The required governmental bookkeeping on the merchant has been reduced to adding up his sales receipts. The work of the IRS has been reduced and limited to auditing the cash receipts register. Expense accounts, depreciation, cost of goods sold, advertising, etc. are business management decisions which are not the concern of the government whose business sense approaches zip.

Interest and dividends would be handled in the same manner as payroll. When interest earned and company profits (dividends) are paid, 10% should go to the Treasury Department and 90% to the client. No need to even list the recipients. The work of the IRS has been reduced to auditing the distribution of interest and profits being paid.

The advantages of this simple system are so numerous I shall only list them without elaboration. If you will spend a little time to think about this simplicity, you will probably come up with even more advantages:

- The nonproductive mathematical gamesmanship would virtually disappear.

- Business expenses (amortization schedules, double declining balances, whether to lease or buy, three martini lunches, charitable donations, advertising, insurance, retirement plans, etc.) would now be the sole concern of business managers and their stockholders and not the Federal Government who hasn't been able to manage its budget for decades.

- Individuals, businesses, and the federal government would all know every month exactly where they stand financially and wouldn't have to wait until April 15 each year to find out.

- Foreign companies doing business here in the United States would pay the same taxes as our domestic companies.

- Domestic products being wholesaled abroad would be tax free, allowing them to be competitive in foreign markets.

- The billions of dollars currently being spent to operate the Internal Revenue Service would be reduced as much as 95% to 99%.

- "Big Brotherism" would be drastically reduced, maybe even a thing of the past. The IRS wouldn't even have a file on individuals.

Although this is a vast improvement over what we have now, it can't be all good, so here is the bad side. There would be literally thousands of bureaucrats, tax accountants, tax lawyers and bookkeepers out looking for meaningful employment. I must admit that all subsidies aren't bad and a few (very few) should be continued but most definitely not in the form of hidden tax deductions. See Chapter 14. If subsidies have to be sneaked past the taxpaying public they are not worth it.

Now that we have removed the IRS from the subsidy business, we'll have to create another branch of the government to handle this task. This new department will employ some of the displaced bureaucrats, and as luck would have it, they are already experienced in the subsidy racket. Under this scheme, all subsidies will be out in the open where they can be totalled, so we can see who is being subsidized and how much they actually cost us. I can picture in my mind some of the debates trying to justify some of these subsidies and the amount of each subsidy which heretofore has been hidden. The people who want subsidies are the only ones who will have to fill out all those governmental forms instead of involving all of us taxpayers in their subsidy problem. The IRS currently has 342 separate forms to play with, which is a stack of paper 4 times as thick as this book, assuming each is only a single page long.

There is another huge advantage to this simplicity. It provides a very simple method of raising and lowering taxes to match governmental spending. If the government spends more than it receives, then the tax rate would be immediately raised so that tax revenues would match government expenditures and vice versa. Every few years we elect (or carelessly re-elect most of the time) members of congress with the hope that things will get better, and then we sit withdrawn, unconcerned, and allow them to continue to spend us further into debt. This has gone on for over fifty years and we never get wiser. If our taxes were adjusted monthly to match government spending, it is highly probable that our congressmen would hear from us on a regular basis in a very loud, clear voice concerning their spending habits. In all probability they would hear us or be replaced in the next election. If we continue to sit back on our complacency we deserve the mess we have now. Congress would be confined to spending our current income instead of the income of the next generation.

Now do yourself a favor by starting your personal letter writing campaign to get congress to replace the income tax with a payroll tax, an earnings tax, and a national sales tax. Get your friends into the act but proceed with great caution in two areas. When your friends get a little glassy-eyed and step back a couple of paces like you might become dangerous at any minute, it's time to change the subject quickly. The other word of caution is a very serious threat. Our big-spending congressmen will probably quickly accept the payroll tax and the national retail sales tax as new sources of income and will continue the current income tax also. This is a real threat not to be taken lightly.

SUMMARY

1. The ONLY legitimate purpose of taxes is to raise money to pay the expenses of our government and is not to rule the populace or manage our economy.

2. Our income tax system has been grossly distorted to include hundreds of hidden subsidies favoring many special interest groups, including foreign businesses. We

have become a nation of bookkeepers, lawyers, bureaucrats and cheaters, wasting time and energy playing a non productive game.

3. The IRS has become a three trillion dollar "non productive" business conducted by 122,000 employees costing us about $6,000,000,000 per year who have been proven to have a failing grade of about 60% when quizzed on their subject matter. If the experts get a failing grade, what chance does an amateur have? Or are we all expected to become experts at this non- productive game?

4. *SOLUTION* — Replace the income tax with a payroll tax, a national sales tax and an earnings tax.

5. Our tax system is a man-made problem and not like the weather and the law of gravity — it can be changed. Write to your congressmen *now* and demand the change!

SEE APPENDIX B FOR ASSISTANCE

Chapter 2

FOOTBALL

Football has changed a great deal during my lifetime, and in many cases the rules committee has sadly confused change with progress, which is a common fault not limited to football rules. In order to appreciate the changes that have occurred and evaluate their significance, let's take a little trip down memory lane for the benefit of those of lesser seniority.

I am so old I can remember when football was a sport played almost entirely in high schools and universities and professional football wasn't really on the scene to any extent. A professional football game that drew a crowd of 3000 or more spectators was a banner day. Fifty years ago some players were still wearing leather helmets, and it wasn't mandatory to wear a helmet even in high school football.

The game was played with an eleven-man team plus some substitute players, and each player played both offense and defense. Any player who was taken out of the game for any reason was not permitted to return to the game until the next quarter of the game. There was a team in Iowa, referred to as the "Iowa Iron Men," who finished a season with the first string players averaging 58-1/2 minutes per game. This meant that there were only one or two substitutions throughout the entire season. The place-kicker, quarterback, punters, etc. played the entire game. Eleven men were a team and the days of specialization of labor had not yet arrived. Today coaches change players like golfers change clubs with a special club for each situation.

The "blitz" (short for *blitzkrieg* which means lightning in German) was a military procedure employed in World War II whereby one military force would throw everything they had at the enemy simultaneously with lightning speed, which usually caused much confusion and panic to their enemy. The blitz applied to football is a maneuver whereby the defense charges almost all their men simultaneously. Some think this is a relatively new tactic, but in reality we have merely gone full circle because this was the only defense known in the early football years.

All plays were required to be called on the field by the quarterback or the team captain and not the brain trusts in business suits on the sidelines or the board of directors located higher in the stadium. Any substitute player sent into the game wasn't allowed to communicate with his teammates in any way until after his first play in the game, which prevented sending plays into the game from the sidelines. Signalling of any kind from the sidelines drew a rather severe penalty. The idea was that two teams were playing each other, not two multifaceted corporations as we have today.

Each team was allowed three time-outs during each half of the game (same as now), but these time-outs were for the purpose of allowing the teams two minutes to rest and get their breath. A time-out was never used to stop the clock, mainly because it was rare to have any time-outs left toward the end of either half of the game because the players were totally exhausted. Furthermore, it was considered poor sportsmanship to stall and refuse to put the ball in play — of course the game was a sport then. During the time-out a "water boy" (now there's a term few fans have ever heard of today) ran onto the field with a bucket of water and a ladle, put them on the ground and quickly removed himself from the area of the players to prevent any suspicion that he had brought in a message from the coaching staff. No player was permitted to converse or communicate in any way with the sidelines during a time-out. If a player required medical attention on the field, an official was present to ensure all conversation with the player was purely medical.

There was no time limit between plays, there was no need for it since the plays were called on the field and substitutions were quite rare. It was also considered good strategy to keep the game moving along rapidly to wear down the opposing team, especially when they showed signs of fatigue.

The football was made of leather with a rubber bladder and was much larger, rounder and heavier than now, and it required a larger than average hand to get a good grip on it, so the game involved far less passing than it does today. Where passing was once quite uncommon, it is now a major part of the game partially due to the size and shape of the ball. Some pass receivers today are already wearing gloves, and if the ball gets any smaller, pass receivers will be recognized by the fielders' mitts they'll be wearing.

The field was marked off in 10-yard increments with no intermediate five yard lines between them or any one yard markers along the sidelines. The officials got pretty good at pacing off penalties one yard per stride. With a small digression you will see why this practice was so suddenly abandoned.

Pacing off penalties was common practice throughout the football world until a game between University of California and St. Marys abruptly changed things. Cal had a huge rooting section consisting of 4000 men in white shirts in the center bordered by two sections of 2000 women each in white blouses, which made for a cohesive, raucous and spontaneous group. When the referee paced off a five-yard penalty, the rooting section helped him count off his paces "1 - 2 - 3 - 4 - 5," and as he placed the ball on the ground they shouted in unison "Y O U B A S T A R D!" This was considered extremely vile language in those days, and the busiest people at the game at that moment were the radio announcers madly throwing switches to prevent such vulgar profanity from going out over the air. On the next play, Cal was again penalized five yards and the whole procedure was repeated, only this time an extra five yard penalty was added for unsportsmanlike conduct in the stands. Cal's coach, Stub Allison, a very popular coach with the student body, requested and was granted an official's time-out to address his rooting section in the stands. His message was polite and jovial stating that these yards on the field come hard and he'd appreciate it very much if the student body wouldn't throw away any more yards. As luck would have it, Cal drew another five yard offsides penalty on the very next play. It appeared, in spite of the coach's pleas, that the procedure was being repeated, starting "1 - 2 - 3 - 4 - 5," but as the official placed the ball on the ground the rooting section broke out in perfect unison singing "For he's a jolly good fellow." *Time Magazine* wrote up the whole incident (with expletive deleted) and that, my children, was the last time an official ever paced off a penalty. Henceforth the officials count the yards on their fingers and point to where the ball should be placed, trot to the spot with choppy little steps and place the ball down with a smirk like they really enjoyed this part of his work.

OK, now back to the "good old days." When the ball went out of bounds for one reason or other, the referee would bring it back onto the field by pacing off five yards from the sidelines. Placement of the ball in this manner allowed a good opportunity for an end run by a sprinter who had almost the entire width of the field in which to maneuver. There's a lot of grass out there on the field, and it made sense to use it all instead of wearing out the center aisle by starting every play in the soggy bare spot in the middle of the field. This also had considerable bearing on play calling if a field goal was contemplated. The official didn't place the ball directly in front of the goal post for the benefit of the kicker. If you wanted the ball in front of the goal posts, you had to call a play that would center it there yourself. Also those automatic field goal chip shots from the five or ten yard line became a real challenge if the ball was near the side lines.

On a punt play there was no such thing as a "fair catch," and the ball was in play until it was either (1) caught by a player on the receiving team who either downed the ball or was tackled, or (2) the ball rolled dead untouched by either team, or (3) an offensive player touched the ball before the receiving team.

There was another kicking option which hasn't been seen for several decades and that is the "drop kick," which was a free ball available to either team to pick up and run with. This wasn't used very often because it was somewhat unreliable, but the potential threat kept the defense alert. Drop kicking, which has become a lost art, was sometimes used for conversions after a touchdown because it provided one more blocker to protect the kicker. Kicking tees and other ancillary equipment did not exist and holding the ball for that kicking machine, who rarely speaks English, was done by a human team player instead of a tee.

When tackling a ball carrier, you could grab him anywhere you wished because there were no face masks.

The nostalgia trip is over now. It was only mentioned here to show how much the game has changed. (Please note I didn't say improved). These changes have taken place over a period of many years, for if they had all occurred in a single year, the name of the game would have been changed from "football" to "corporate computerball" or some other descriptive name because the foot is now of minor significance. Today's game has so many rules and officials that the play-off games have seven officials on the field plus a few more in the replay booth surrounded by electronic gadgets with infallible memories which allow a questionable play to be reviewed from many angles an infinite number of times by a higher court before a conference is held to determine how to proceed. Consequently, it has become quite difficult to complete more than a couple of consecutive plays without a penalty, and the officials aren't even calling all the rules violations. In the second Houston Oilers/Cleveland Browns game in 1988, there were 121 successful plays totalling 586 yards (not counting punts and runbacks) with 22 penalties totaling 193 yards. This figures out to 32.9% of all movements of the ball were made by the officials instead of the players. The situation is really much worse than these figures indicate because they do not include the penalties that were refused. Is this what we came to see? The game is degenerating to the point where we will soon leave the uniformed players at home and send out a group of lawyers in business suits with brief cases representing each team who will get together with the officials and inform us in the newspapers of the winners after several appeals a few weeks later. Who needs grass for a game like this?

Even with all these officials referee, Jerry Seeman, the official in charge of this mess, said after a game that one of his officials (Ray Dodez) missed a call that cost Cleveland a touchdown and the victory. Sorry about the embarrassment, Ray, but I've got to prove a point. With all these officials calling so many penalties there was scarcely a single penalty for unsportsmanlike conduct. Thomas M. Burnet, United Press International, said,

> The Oilers, the most penalized team in the NFL, and the Browns played as if they were battling for the chance at a World Wrestling Federation title rather an NFL championship. As for fights, Houston coach Jerry Glanville was flippant when asked to comment and was quoted as saying "Were there a lot of fights? We don't care about penalties today. We'll take this win just the way it is.

At another time he was heard to say words to the effect that we don't feel we've been in a football game if we didn't lose at least 100 yards in penalties.

On several occasions two or more players were called for fighting during the game. The officials awarded them offsetting penalties with the result that nobody was penalized, which is tantamount to condoning fighting. If we don't straighten out the officials and coaching staffs with stiffer penalties, it is obvious the players will never change. Professional wrestling with all its ballyhoo is rapidly creeping into football.

A couple more quotes from *United Press International* drive my point home even further.

The referees did not take control of the game early. Despite pushing matches that started early in the game, no penalty was called in such a situation until late in the second quarter.

Six days earlier, the Browns defeated the Oilers, 28-23, a game marred by snowballs and dog bones tossed at Houston players by fans in the end zone bleacher section.

Saturday, several dozen police officers were on hand to prevent a repeat, but it may have been better if they had been looking toward the field instead of the bleachers

In the Cleveland / Cincinnati game a player deliberately hit an official in the chest and was not ejected from the game. The incident definitely called for a penalty for unsportsmanlike conduct or ejection from the game. On the next seven consecutive plays the Cincinnati players either hit or shoved an opposing player after the whistle had blown the play dead without a single penalty.

The announcers and sports writers are contributing to this degeneration of what was once a sport. Words like tackle and block are outmoded and have been replaced by hit, physical, rung his bell, BAM!, sock'em, etc. It isn't necessary to kill, injure or maim an opposing player by throwing your body through the air at him as hard as possible so he'll remember you next time and then looking around for accolades of praise from your buddies and the coaching staff. The idea is to stop the ball carrier. It has been my observation that special punting teams charge the potential runback specialist so hard that they miss him completely the overwhelming majority of the time. I've never known any player who could change his direction of travel with his feet off the ground. It is rare to see a tackler get in front of a runback specialist and delay him long enough for help to arrive to tackle him. The number one assignment for a defensive end is to make ABSOLUTELY and EMPHATICALLY certain that the ball carrier does not run between him and the sidelines. He must direct the play so that his teammates can also participate in preventing forward progress of the ball carrier. The problem here is that praise from the fans and announcers comes with those occasionally sensational tackles that flatten somebody in his own backfield with all the fanfare of Roman gladiators. With announcers and coaches counting successful "sacks," why should any player stay home in his position and do what his number one assignment calls for when his successes are remembered long after his failures?

We have all experienced bad days where absolutely nothing goes right and an occasional good day where we can't make a mistake. I've had golf scores that range from 83 to about 120 plus, which really proves my point. Quarterbacks are no different (I'm not talking about their golf scores) so why don't the coaches take them out of the game when they are having a bad day? The answer I get from some people is that it would destroy the morale of the quarterback. I doubt that leaving him in the game to humiliate himself helps his morale very much either. Another answer I get is that it's hard for his team to adjust to the idiosyncrasies and timing of a new quarterback. Yep! It probably is, but it is just as hard for the defense to adjust, which is another plus for changing quarterbacks. How can I be so brilliant to see this when those coaches being paid over a million dollars per year can't see it?

While it's the coaches turn in the barrel, let's question why they suddenly change to an unsuccessful running game on the three-yard line when they got down there with ten successful passing plays? And then there's the "prevent defense." The object of the prevent defense is to let the opposing team catch up with your score slowly and hope they don't pass up your score before the end of the game. Dumb! They should rename it the "defeat defense" because that's where it usually leads.

Now that I've beaten to death the faults of the game (in my opinion) it's time to make some constructive criticisms and suggestions. Let's take the easiest ones first.

There is absolutely no justification for fighting and there should be no such thing as offsetting penalties for fighting. Fighting is not a judgment call, so let's just make it an automatic penalty of suspension from the current game and possibly a few following games without pay and the player not allowed in the stadium or practice field during this period. Too severe? Maybe, but it would be instantly effective as soon as this rule was properly explained to a few players in public. This should in no way detract from the game and those who want to see fights are free to spend their evenings at boxing matches, hockey games, and wrestling exhibitions where the object of the game appears to be to injure or render your opponent helpless. Poor sportsmanship has reached a point where Notre Dame doesn't even wait for the game to begin, but attacks the visiting team in the players' tunnel.

Unnecessary roughness is a little tougher because it's a judgment call by the officials, when and if they choose to see it. There is a substantial difference between the pat on the head I give my grandson and a blow intended to deliver my opponent into silly land. Admittedly, the officials on the field cannot see everybody all the time but the boys in the booth full of electronic toys have a full view of the playing field and should be permitted a voice in the matter. Furthermore, they are safe up there in their booth and the players can't even argue with them. When unnecessary roughness is called, a severe penalty should be applied to both the player and the team. Peer pressure from a penalized team would have and immediate, emphatic effect on the player. I would suggest removal from the team for a game or two. A player who is unable to control himself is not worth much to the owners of the club, his team or himself. This being a judgment call, there should be penalties ranging from immediate ejection from the game, locker room and stadium up to ejection from football as a career. These penalties might sound too severe, but keep in mind they would be extremely rare after the players, coaches and owners got the hang of it.

Now let's talk about the size of the field. It's pretty hard to make an end run in a narrow alley, so let's return a ball that has gone out-of-bounds only a few yards inside the playing field instead of the middle of the field. This would also tighten up on some of those automatic chip shot field goals and add a little strategy to the game. Let those super specialists (millionaires who never get their uniforms dirty) earn those gigantic salaries by kicking field goals from a few yards inside the field sidelines instead of directly in front of the goal posts.

If you were the world's second best quarterback playing behind the world's greatest quarterback, it would be doubtful that you would ever play in a game. What a waste of talent. Maybe quarterbacks should be limited to three quarters of play per game, particularly in high school and college games.

The field would be effectively enlarged if a pass receiver were considered in the field of play until he put a foot down outside the playing field. This would effectively widen the field at least one full stride on each side and the end zone netting about ten or twelve additional feet of playing field in all directions.

OK, now here comes my real pet peeve. The clock. If we came to see two teams play sixty minutes of football, we are just kidding ourselves. What we really see is 13 minutes and 20 seconds of football and 46 minutes and 40 seconds of watching the teams huddle, officials walking around the field with the ball in their hands, and quarterbacks either kneeling on one knee or standing there watching the clock run down. Time a game with a stop watch only from the snap of the ball to the whistle that blows the play dead. Having timed many games, I was amazed that the actual playing time of several games was within a percent or two of the average of 13 minutes and 20 seconds, which totals exactly 800 seconds per game. Let's have four 200-second quarters with the clock running only while the ball is in play. If game time were kept this way, the officials could walk around the field on their own time. Players who stall by slowly walking back to the huddle, the slow huddle, slow signal calling and dropping on one knee could not penalize the opponent. Stalling should not be permitted as a weapon. A team should be required to beat their opposition playing ball rather than *not* playing ball. Forget the stalling and lets play ball for a change!

As spectators we are very much a part of the game. This is affirmed weekly by the professional gambling odds makers making allowances in the score for the home field advantage. Even though the spectators are a significant part of the team, they are required to stay in the stands and not interfere with the game on the field. Not interfering with the game should include not throwing objects such as bottles, beer, snowballs, dog bones, soft drinks and other debris, or using huge horns and mechanical noise makers intended to intimidate the opposing players, or in any way interfering with the game. The police could handle this situation in a militaristic manner. A far more practical way, though, would be to penalize the team with which the spectators have aligned. Obviously, a fan or two who get overly exuberant should be benched outside the stadium in a militaristic fashion, but other measures closer to home come to mind. For instance, a player shouldn't be permitted to stand up facing the fans and wave his arms or towels in a circle over his head making himself an unofficial cheer leader pleading for more fan noise to prevent his opponents from hearing their signals. Players on the field also should cease gesturing with arms outstretched, the flats of their hands raised up signalling for more noise. The huge TV screen at the end of the field should not be allowed to flash "NOISE — MORE NOISE." Is there no limit to poor sportsmanship? In this area of poor sportsmanship, the ultimate was the coach of the Chicago Bears who urged in the local newspaper the day before the game for the fans to come and "get more involved in the game earlier, tomorrow." This poor sport has now been inducted into the Football Hall of Fame, so I guess this is considered acceptable behavior. With so many games being played in greenhouses (enclosed stadia), the noise factor becomes increasingly important. Wouldn't it be nice if coaches and players exhibited some good sportsmanship by gesturing for a little quiet from their fans for their opponents. Maybe a time-out charged against the defense might help get the point across. If the appeal for good sportsmanship fails, I suggest a ten minute cooling-off period should be called by the officials whereby all players would leave the field and return to finish the game without a few unofficial cheer leaders who didn't get the message earlier.

When the communications link between the top of the stadium and the bench is disrupted for one team, the officials re-

quire that the telephones be shut off for the other team to prevent an unfair advantage. Why can't the same procedure be applied to signal calling. If one team is prevented from hearing their
quarterback's signals, then the other team should be prohibited
from calling signals likewise.

If something isn't done by the rules committee, I'd recommend that every traveling team take with them a huge brass band
with lots of drums and amplifiers as standard equipment so the
home team can't hear their quarterback's signals either. OK, Don
Shula and others on the rules committee, let's talk sportsmanship now before things get too far out of hand like European
soccer. Put the game back on the field and out of the stands.

On March 21, 1989 (four months after this chapter was
first written) I am pleased to report that the NFL met
in Palm Desert and approved a new rule 21 to 7 to curb
the noise to protect the visiting team. After two warn-
ings, the home team will be penalized by losing a time-
out or a five-yard penalty if they have no time-outs left.
My confidence is slowly being restored.

Up to now I stand four square behind my recommendations
and feel they should be seriously adopted. The next category is
just food for thought, which might be a little harder to defend.
These I'll call my "what-ifs."

What-if — every player was eligible to catch a pass? There
would probably be more agile players playing on the line and the
days of the sumo wrestlers would be limited. It would be a much
faster game with far fewer injuries.

What-if — there were no such thing as an incomplete pass
and the ball is in play until picked up by a player? Any ball that
is thrown out-of-bounds would go over to the opposition where

it went out-of-bounds, same as a punt. Any incomplete pass on fourth down would go over to the opposition at the point of origin of the play.

What-if — there were a weight limit on the size of the players permitted to play the game, say 240 pounds? There would be fewer injuries by such weight mismatches as 300 or more pounds vs. 180 pounds or less.

What-if — every penalty, no matter how trivial, carried with it a minimum of either a gain or loss of one down, depending on whether it was on the offense or defense?

The what-ifs are fun to imagine and talk about, but they shouldn't be allowed to distract us from the more serious, practical and desperately needed changes in the game now.

Chapter 3

NARCOTICS

We (excluding criminals, racketeers, sadists, idiots, the uninformed and the misinformed) are probably pretty much in agreement on most issues regarding narcotics. They are not healthy for us and should not be used unless prescribed by a physician for medicinal purposes only. They are ruining a large number of both our youth and adults. They have directly caused much grief through broken homes. They have destroyed many people financially. They have given us the largest criminal society of all time. The list can go on and on, which would be beating a dead horse since we all agree on these matters. I can make this statement without fear of contradiction for those who would disagree with it certainly are not reading this book.

Probably the only disagreement we have is what to do about the situation. The majority of those with whom I have talked and listened agree that what we are currently doing is not effective enough to do the job we want done. In other words we are definitely losing the war on drugs. I mean no disrespect to those hard-working and diligent people fighting this war on our behalf and giving it their all. My criticism is for the unenforced laws, judges, criminal lawyers, crooked politicians, foreign governments, etc. who are not helping, or, even worse, are contributing to the problem.

The situation is really getting desperate. The problem has reached such epidemic proportions that approaches to this problem once considered ridiculous and impractical are now worth serious investigation. The first idea that comes to mind is to legalize dope to take the profit motive out of it. I am told that extremely expensive illegal drugs in today's drug market could be produced dirt cheap by our current pharmaceutical firms if made legally. Importers and home laboratories would not be able to compete with the price and quality of professionally produced drugs and still make a profit. Our current effort and expense of fighting the drug war could be directed toward educating present drug addicts and soon to become drug addicts on the dangers of drugs. At least this scheme would remove the illegal street vendors from the scene and virtually bankrupt the criminal gangs associated with the illicit drug business now. Who knows? It might even reduce muggings, prostitution, many murders, home break-ins and have a beneficial effect on the AIDS menace.

Maybe if we gave this idea a six month or one year try we would find some good results. We would have to give it a long enough try to drive out or dry up the current illicit drug trade. I shudder at the thought that the idea might backfire and result in a much larger number of addicts. It is shocking how misunderstood this approach is with our press. One of our TV reporters thinks it is a sound idea to legalize drugs so we can tax them heavily to get money to educate people on the dangers of drugs.

Maybe after he has had time to think it over he will realize that he has just reintroduced the criminal element right back into the scheme of things by smuggling and selling tax free drugs at a lower price.

After giving the idea much thought several side effects come to mind that are both good and bad. The first bad feature has already been mentioned, which is that we may end up with more drug addicts than we started with. I can hear people justifying their harmful habits by saying they must be all right since they're endorsed by the Government's Food and Drug Administration. The next side effect that pops into mind is that with such cheap and available drugs we would become an exporter of addictive drugs and be damned by the world in the same manner as Colombia and several other countries are damned by us now. If our own drug addict population grows, it is very likely that our exporting cheap drugs would contribute to the increase of the world-wide drug addict population. It's beginning to sound about as practical as putting out a fire with gasoline. If we try this idea on an experimental basis, we must (I repeat MUST) have a foolproof scheme waiting to be implemented to stop this experiment as soon as it becomes obvious that it is getting out of hand. If all drug addicts were required to register to buy their cheap drugs at least we would know who they are when it came time to terminate the experiment. I can see the addict list now — three million John Smiths, three million Mickey Mouses (or is it Mice?), one million Mary Jones and the remainder made up of Ben Franklins, Eleanor Roosevelts and one Jimmie Carter (sorry Jimmie, it just wasn't your year). This could turn out to be the ultimate Pandora's Box and should not be approached with reckless abandon. Merely studying and thinking about it is not for the weak-hearted or the trepid.

While studying the consequences of some of the more drastic solutions, I recommend we keep the laws the way they are at present but change our philosophy and the emphasis of our efforts. The current emphasis consists of throwing most of our effort into trying to dry up the supply of drugs. Unfortunately, this approach has resulted in more crime, better organized crime gangs, more addicts, more dope smuggling, more illegal drug laboratories and more street vendors. In many large cities the vendors are so thick they are fighting to get to the customers (addicts) and are stumbling all over each other (or their corpses). One has to become thoroughly anesthetized with drugs just to get enough courage to walk through these areas. It has reached a point where the sales of Ouzi machine guns is rivaling the sales of narcotics.

The amazing part of all this is that our law enforcement personnel have any morale left considering the circumstances under which they are working now. I'm referring to the ACLU, the labor unions, the professional athletes, government workers, railroad employees, airline employees, etc. protecting the drug addicts by fighting against drug testing. The situation is similar to squeezing a bubble on a balloon and watching the bubble pop out somewhere else on the balloon, or cutting off one strand of crab grass and finding that two have replaced it almost immediately. Every day we read in the newspapers of the "largest drug bust ever." We silently say to ourselves "so what" because we know this record will not hold up long and will be broken many times in the very near future. Headlines like this have become so routine they have no impact on us any more. In Oakland, California, after many months of hard dangerous undercover work, over 150 drug peddlers were picked up in one night's raid. Over 100 of them were back on the street in less than three hours

NARCOTICS

due to lack of jail facilities. The officers participating in the raid knew this would happen, yet they pursued their job diligently. How long can we expect such devotion from them without giving them more support? The local news medium expressed pleasant surprise that those arrested weren't all out of jail immediately.

Everybody should be drug tested, including all professional athletes, government workers, employees, etc. There are automatic fines for drivers who refuse to take an alcohol test, so why not drug users too? The NFL, major league baseball, etc. have a policy of suspending players who use drugs. Phooey! The US has a policy too. If you use illegal drugs you are punished by the state. It sort of narrows down to — are we going to enforce the law or not. Drug testing should be done with a U.S. marshall standing by. If the NFL and major league baseball players refuse to play if they must be drug tested let them take their habits and go home and try to make a living at something else. It is doubtful their new income would be a fraction of the salary they just walked away from. For every player who walks away from a million dollar paycheck there are literally hundreds who would cheerfully replace him or her. If all insurance companies were to require a drug test before issuing an automobile related policy (and I think they should) drug use would suddenly diminish dramatically.

There seems to be a deterioration of our morals. What's OK? A little bit of corruption, a little bit of smuggling, a little bit of crime, a little bit of drug use, or what? Using or possessing drugs is illegal, but a few ounces found on a person has become acceptable.

Any solid citizens who are not aware of the problem are either closely related to Rip Van Winkle or are new arrivals from outer space, so there is no need to describe the problem further. So what shall we do differently?

It's back to the old supply and demand theory, which has been so successfully employed in the business community. Let's face it, this is really big business. I say change the emphasis from trying to dry up the supply to trying to dry up the demand. I say change the emphasis and not abandon the current programs. Let's do a little environmental impact study on this idea to see where it leads.

First of all, it is far less dangerous to arrest drug users because they rarely carry Ouzi machine guns, do not travel in large organized gangs, commit murders and are so unsophisticated in criminal matters they are sitting ducks very easy to find. Many can be found by merely reading the newspapers. Now that we have a few million potential prisoners on our hands, we have an even larger problem as to what to do with them. Punishment for their crimes cannot be uniform because they are not uniform people. Those who have jobs, families and an income could be given progressive fines, starting with a good hand-slapping and progressing up to some really big bucks on successive offenses. Some should be incarcerated for varying periods of time long enough to at least temporarily kick the habit. A little time off should be granted for the drug addict for assisting in the incarceration of their drug peddler. A few hundred or thousand hours of public service work would be beneficial to all, particularly if served in narcotic wards of hospitals or drug rehabilitation clinics where they can observe the agonies of their fellow drug addicts kicking the habit. House arrest with an electronic surveillance anklet is another possible penalty which carries with it the shame from one's peers without interfering with their ability to earn a living or shop for necessities. This punishment also has the benefit that we do not have to house, feed and guard them. In some cases a combination of several of these penalties might be appropriate.

The facilities, laws, and procedures, are all in place and available to us now except for a few hundred thousand jail cells. With a little cooperation from the Feds, we could borrow and utilize abandoned military bases. Some of these bases aren't yet abandoned so they must be in pretty good working order. After all, these facilities are good enough for honest hard working soldiers who are good citizens. So why should dishonest drug addicts be given anything better? The Armed Forces are not strangers at guarding prisoners and with a little more help from the Feds we have our prison guards who are already on our pay-roll.

Seeking out drug users might become the most over-worked law enforcement job ever. For a real good chuckle just imagine a few hundred narcs (that's "in talk" for Narcotics Officer of the DEA) walking the streets, airports, bus stations, and shopping malls with those cute and playful drug sniffing dogs. At the sight of a person walking a dog on a leash, large groups of people would part like a herd of sheep when a horseman rides through them. Such a sight might even start a panic in some quarters. This scheme may have another pleasant side effect in large cities that have a parking problem. With all of the drug users in hiding, an honest person shouldn't have any problem finding a parking place. Another side effect would be that all the dogs in the animal shelters would be adopted by people who see the advantages of walking around with a dog on a leash like a narcotics officer. No one would know if the dog is narcotics trained and drug users wouldn't stick around to find out. Enough of this nonsense, let's return to reality before some readers think this is all a joke.

After we have talked and studied this thing to death we should do something more than we are doing now. What are you doing?

Chapter 4

PRISONS

It pleases me to say I have absolutely no first hand experience or inside insight of our prison system. This does not preclude me from having an opinion on the subject nor does it disqualify me from talking about it. I do hear many alarming stories about prisons that leave me with the strong impression there is a very definite need to make some corrections to our correctional system. Some of the things I hear are so alarming that if they are only half true they must be corrected immediately. For some reason, women's prisons don't seem to get as much play in the press, so I'll confine this discussion to men's prisons although everything said here would apply equally to both sexes.

Analyzing the problem begins by starting with the question why these people are in prison? It is obvious that they have committed crimes against society and the courts have decided to punish them for their acts and secondly to isolate them from the rest of us for our sake. Here again comes one of those "I heards" where I am unable to quote my source. I heard that the prison population is 78% functionally illiterate. Another "I heard" contradicts this fact only slightly stating that the average educational level of prisoners is the fourth grade. In either case, it is obvious that the inmates are there because they do not have the education, self-respect and confidence to make an honest living in our society even if they wanted. This only means that they are uneducated — not dumb.

Psychologists have experimented with rats and other animals and definitely determined that those who live in an overcrowded society become very belligerent to those around them. These overcrowded conditions in our prisons push the prisoners back in the direction from which they came. This doesn't sound very productive to me, and furthermore, I get the feeling the prisoners will eventually return to the streets a little more experienced in criminal matters and a little tougher than they were when they were sent there. Who wins under these conditions? About the only good I can see is that society has a brief respite while the criminal element is isolated from us at tax payers' expense and a few people are employed as guards. It hardly seems worth it for what we are getting. Here again the situation sounds so desperate that something must be done much differently than it is being done now. Furthermore we can't do things much worse than we are doing them now, which justifies a little experimentation.

Let's start with the court system that put these people there for a prescribed length of time. Remember when we were kids and our parents dealt us some pretty strong punishment on occasion and then eased off a little at a later date? This taught us to always expect leniency. We have learned that we can beat the system and when punishment is dealt out — ha! — they don't really mean it — they just talk tough. Five years, bologna, I'll be out in 18 months or less. Life sentence without the possibility of parole? Hardly, or at least, very rarely. Let's make some changes in the prison sentences.

While we're on the subject, let's digress a minute to cover the death penalty. There are 240 prisoners on death row in California who I presume are all murderers. Since every serial or repeat killer started his killing spree with one killing that makes every one of those on death row potentially a serial or repeat killer. Capital punishment is definitely a deterrent to crime because if every murderer were given immediate capital punishment after his first killing, he could never have an opportunity for his second killing or a killing spree thus saving many lives. This is an irrefutable fact that even California's former supreme court judges and those against the death penalty can't disagree. There hasn't been an execution in California in twelve years thanks to an ultra liberal supreme court that took the law into their own hands in spite of their oath of office that said they would support and enforce *our* laws — not *their* laws. I scoff at those who say it is cheaper to keep a man in jail for life than to off him and be done with it. Show me. And that covers that subject quite thoroughly, so now back to the subject of sentencing.

Sentences should be in three parts. The first part would consist of time to be served which would remove the culprit from society for a prescribed length of time for our protection. The second part of the sentence would be directed at correcting the problem that put the man there in the first place: His lack of education which resulted in his inability to make an honest living and get along in our society. For instance, after examining the convicted offender, the sentence might be five years confinement *AND* an educational requirement that the man must not be released until he has successfully achieved a prescribed academic goal (e.g. an eighth grade examination in English). The sentence would vary depending upon the severity of his crime, the length of his incarceration and his current academic level. Every criminal sentenced to more than one year should lose his citizenship and the absolute minimum requirement for any prisoner serving one year or longer should be that the prisoner pass the United States Citizenship examination in English before his release. This is the requirement for those entering our society from a foreign country to become citizens, so I see no reason why should we expect any less from those entering our society from a prison. If ignorance or lack of education put them there in the first place, then let's see to it that it is not ignorance or lack of education that returns them there.

I stress that everything must be in English, for our laws, street signs, directions, ballots, income tax forms, newspapers, TV news casts, etc., are all in English, and those who cannot read and write our basic language are severely handicapped.

We all know that education requires a lot of time and money. Time certainly is not a problem for the prisoner so we can dispense with that immediately. Money normally would be required for books, school rooms, teachers and supplies. Yes, books and supplies might be a problem, if the prisons don't print their own books. I can hear the book publishers around the nation screaming now that we are muscling in on their business but this is business they didn't have in the first place, so what harm has been done? As for classrooms, I can recall the military using mess halls and tents for classrooms. I can even recall universities using tents on the lawns when crowded conditions called for it.

Now as for teachers, it is quite probable that we can recruit some teachers within the prison population. This is where the third part of the prisoner's sentence comes in. Along with punitive lock up time and the educational requirement, each prisoner's sentence should include a prescribed amount of "public service" time. This time can be served in or out of prison at the courts' pleasure. We have some minimum security, white collar prisons full of very well-educated men who could use some public service time. Teachers might come from some of those narcotics offenders in Chapter Three who need to work off some public service time. This would be a kind of bootstrap situation where teachers would teach some prisoners to become teachers who ultimately teach the prisoner students. After the prisoner teachers have fulfilled their prison sentences, they might even return to our society as experienced teachers. We need them. With a little pushing and shoving and cooperation, it could be made to work quite inexpensively. We must not overlook the economics and feasibility of having a computer terminal as standard equipment in every prison cell. Floppy disks are much cheaper than books, and furthermore, those who are not familiar with computers are going to be severely handicapped in the next generation.

Now with regard to those crowded conditions that turn little rats into big rats, we simply need more prisons. Things have really become desperate. There for a while we heard of prisoners being freed by judges because the prisons were too crowded, and now it has reached a point where they don't even lock them up initially, like the 150 dope peddlers arrested in Oakland who were booked and sent to "Go" without "going directly to jail" as the game of Monopoly so simply states it. This subject was covered in the last chapter by utilizing abandoned, or scheduled to be abandoned, military bases. Two shining examples in California are the Presidio in San Francisco and Mather Air Force Base in Sacramento. In addition to these two examples there are 85 other bases around the country about to be abandoned.

The Presidio in San Francisco is 1,526 acres, which is more than enough room for the 5,290 people currently working there. It includes hospital facilities, barracks, etc. Some of the land is not usable, such as the cemetery and maybe the golf course, but the remainder sounds pretty good for our purposes.

Mather Air Force Base in Sacramento has 5,845 acres (a little more than nine square miles) with 3,000 people currently working there. Here again, it is not all usable space, but of the nine square miles we should be able to find some usable space and buildings for our prison requirements.

Everything needed to try this scheme on an experimental basis is currently available, so let's go. What have we lost if the scheme fails miserably? It is most probable that some group like the ACLU will say this idea is imposing on the prisoners' rights, or maybe it's considered cruel or unusual punishment to require the uneducated to better themselves. If mandatory education is legal for children, it certainly shouldn't be too tough for prisoners. I posed this idea to a lady who had an administrative position in a prison. She told me the idea was illegal under the present laws and doubted very much that we could get the laws changed. Someplace, somewhere, and somehow there is somebody who knows how to set up an experimental program of this nature which could prove or disprove the worthiness of this plan. It is possible that some prisoners would like to volunteer for the experimental program.

It is hopeful that this expanded prison system would be a

temporary situation, for if it is successful, the prison population should shrink immeasurably for lack of repeat offenders. I repeat, what have we to lose?

Let's give this triple pronged prison sentence a name like TRI-SENTENCE and start a bumper sticker campaign to initiate an experiment. Can't you see the bumper stickers now?

TRY TRI

If you can find the right pressure points in the penal system, please let me know so I can donate a few copies of this chapter of the book where it will do the most good.

Chapter 5

LAWYERS & THE LEGAL PROFESSION

Did you notice this chapter is entitled "Lawyers and the Legal Profession" and does not mention justice? That is an entirely different subject (I'm very sorry to say). The opinions on lawyers probably vary from state to state, but since I live in California, the super-saturated lawyer capital of the world, my views are probably quite a bit stronger than those who live in more friendly and peaceful communities. I have forgotten the exact numbers but I do recall that there are more lawyers per thousand people in California than any other state in the Union. Furthermore, the United States has more lawyers per thousand of the population than any other nation in the world. WHY? I have heard that the United States has over one hundred times as many lawyers per thousand people than Japan. I also heard that Japan has only about 10,000 lawyers in their entire country, which is probably less than some of our cities.

The legal profession is a huge game being played like any

other sport such as chess, where men are forced to fight one another and are sacrificed for the benefit of the player. There are written rules and some unwritten rules, and the game is closed to all outsiders (those of us who have chosen to make an honest living, have not passed the bar examination and who write on 8 1/2" X 11" paper). The rules of this game are written by lawyers and describe what the players can do with the pawns (that's you and me). One of Webster's definitions of pawn is "one that can be used often to his own disadvantage to further the purposes of another." Another definition is "in the hands of those who thrive on agitation and unrest — Elijah."

Unfortunately, lawyers create the need for more lawyers. If I recall the numbers correctly, California got close to 2,000 new lawyers last year and over 1,800 new laws. As long as lawyers talk a different language full of whereas's, heretofore's, notwithstanding's, and parties dealing with parties instead of people, we must deal with lawyers to interpret what other law-yers are saying. Have you ever noticed that ambiguity seems to increase by the square of the number of words used? Abraham Lincoln was a real disgrace to the legal profession when he wrote his famous Gettysburg Address. Any other lawyer could easily have covered the subject most adequately with 150,000 words or more.

That band of lawyers sometimes referred to as the legislature goes merrily about its business of pontificating and passing new laws without a thought about who is going to enforce the laws. Could it be that they are under the impression that our law en-forcement establishment is just sitting around waiting for some new laws so they will have something to do? Maybe it should be mandatory that every new law carry with it an appropriation to cover the costs to enforce it, and when the money runs out so does the law. A law that is not enforced or just partially enforced encourages crime. Maybe that's the answer — to just make laws and forget about enforcing them. The problem has been with us literally for centuries and continues to get worse with an unpredictable end — a truly revolting thought. England has been making laws ten times longer than we have, and yet they have less than one tenth the number of laws. While the people of Europe are throwing off their shackles, we should ponder the shackles we voluntarily accept in our daily lives. California has enacted 14,899 laws since 1981. At this rate, in 10 more years we'll have 15,000 more state laws than we now have. These laws are in addition to all of our current laws and to all the laws of the federal, county, and city governments. Will we be more or less free? (See Chapter 9 — Sunset Laws)

Was it Socrates, Plato, Caesar, or Brutus who said , "First we have to get rid of all the lawyers?"

The legal profession is almost unique in that it gets paid a handsome bonus for its inefficiency. In this regard lawyers are very cooperative with each other. The longer the case can be drawn out, the more prosperous for both the lawyers (alleged adversaries). Several years ago I was being deposed by a very belligerent lawyer who ended up in a heated debate with my lawyer. They mutually agreed to discontinue the deposition and take the matter to "law and motion." When asked, my lawyer said this is a special court where lawyers go before a judge to settle a matter of principle of law. In spite of my lawyer's very strong objections, I went to "law and motion" with him after I reminded him that I was paying the bills and this was all new to me and I wanted to know what was going on. Just as he had told me, I didn't understand what was being said by either lawyer or the judge. Finally my lawyer turned away from the judge's bench with a smile and motioned for me to meet him in the hall saying, "We won! We won!" "What did we win?" I stupidly asked. "We got a two months continuation." My reply to him was, "We won? Hell, that only means you're on my payroll for another two months. Hell man, get this thing settled. This isn't a football game or soccer game, this is my future you're playing with. Everything I own is at stake here." We never had a civil conversation thereafter. The lawyers managed to drag out the case thirty-three months at their clients' expense.

When lawyers are picking a jury, they disqualify almost all engineers because engineers think in terms of black or white. Lawyers deal in an infinite number of shades of gray.

Have you ever noticed that all witnesses who testify in a courtroom or on a deposition are sworn to tell the truth, the jury is sworn in, the plaintiff, the defendants, everybody who speaks in court is sworn in — except the lawyers who are free to speculate as to the truth and who lie repeatedly in the form of accusations? Dr. Goebels, head of the Propaganda Ministry for the Third Reich, taught us in World War II that if you repeat a ridiculous lie enough times people will start to believe you.

And then there is the matter of "inadmissible evidence." Apple sauce! Either it happened or it didn't happen. If it happened or didn't happen, those are facts. If we are to have any justice, all pertinent facts must be made known. If the evidence was obtained illegally, then the law breaker who obtained the evidence illegally should be punished appropriately, but pretending that the evidence doesn't exist and reward some potentially guilty person by withholding this evidence falls in the general category of childish stupidity. This seems so elementary to me I fail to see why this is controversial.

Having been very harsh on lawyers and the whole legal system in general, I must admit the major portion of my vindictive wrath is directed toward trial lawyers. There is definitely a need for some contract lawyers in our society. This stems from the fact that we didn't learn in school how to express our thoughts very succinctly for all to understand. Our normal means of communication is based on much slang, arm waving, ambiguous terms and punctuated by lots of "ya-knows" and "see what I means?". Many times when I was negotiating contracts, we had a great deal of conversation discussing what work was going to be accomplished or how the product would perform which ended up with a meeting of the minds as to what the contract should say. When we all agreed, the job was done. To summarize what we had agreed to, I'd write it on a blackboard in the conference room, which resulted in many concurrences and many disagreements. Obviously we had not communicated. One of our corporate officers had a framed plaque on the wall saying:

"MAKE THE DEAL *BEFORE* YOU SIGN THE CONTRACT."

Straightening out this legal mess has some monumental hurdles which may be too high to be conquered. The first hurdle is that we are asking the law makers, who are lawyers, to straighten out lawyers. I don't think their fraternal code permits their tampering with the good thing they have going for them. The second hurdle is that the day is rapidly approaching when the lawyers will have us outnumbered, and when that day comes, our chances of straightening out the legal profession will degenerate from absolutely terrible to completely impossible.

I don't know the answers to these problems, but I'll make a feeble attempt at a beginning of a solution.

Let's do away with the "everything to gain — nothing to

lose" approach to suing everybody. If the plaintiff in a civil lawsuit loses, he should be required to pay all the legal expenses of the defendant plus all his other costs associated with the lawsuit. This should have a clearing effect on the court calendar. Also, it might be a good idea if the losing plaintiff's lawyer not be paid, and he should share any losses.

Another possibility. When we need a lawyer, put the job out for bid and sign a binding performance contract with the lawyer including a liquidated damages clause where his fees are diminished if satisfactory performance isn't achieved by an agreed-upon date. This binding contract would be arbitrated by non lawyers. This idea, or one similar, would revolutionize the lawyer business and introduce a degree of efficiency never before dreamed of in the system.

I understand that getting a court date in England takes less than two weeks, whereas it's three or four years here. If this is true, let's study their system well. They must be doing something right that we aren't doing.

If we are to have speedy justice in our criminal courts, we must first do away with the conflict of interest that currently exists. Lawyers should not be allowed to prosper by dragging out trials with numerous continuations and appeals. Give a little thought to this idea.

If a criminal pleads guilty there should be no trial, and sentencing should be carried out within a week by the judge. But on the other hand, if he pleads "not guilty" and is proven guilty in a trial at a later date, his sentence would be substantially increased for having lied to the court. It is truly stupid for a criminal to plead "not guilty" when the crime was performed in front of many witnesses and sometimes recorded on a television camera and on occasion witnessed by millions. This procedure would really put the lawyer on the spot, because if a lawyer permits his client to plead guilty, he has just put himself out of a job. Heaven forbid this should ever happen. The lawyer not only lost the trial job but the many appeals to follow. What a shame!

Crimes committed by lawyers, law enforcement people and elected politicians should carry a much heavier penalty because they are supposed to set good examples and know the laws better than the average citizen.

As long as our laws and our entire legal system is in the hands of lawyers, we are completely at their mercy. This will continue until we can find some way put non lawyers above lawyers. Maybe a law degree should disqualify anyone as a legislator. This sounds like a ridiculous idea but something must be done.

Who or what is the "Bar Association" that seems to set the standards? I don't recall ever voting for them, but they seem to be a ruling body.

WHAT ARE YOUR SUGGESTIONS?

Chapter 6

DOCTORS

After I've had my say about doctors, I'll probably be in the market for some new ones who have never heard of this book. Doctor is a general category which includes Family Practitioners, Internists, Surgeons, Allergists, Optometrists, Ophthalmologists, Dentists, Periodontists, Dermatologists, etc. Holy Smokes! I've seen all these in the past five years, and I consider myself to be in very good health. I only mention this long list because every time I see a new doctor I have to fill out that stupid form. When one doctor sends me to another doctor the first thing is to fill out that damned form. One day when I was unusually annoyed by the doctors' forms, the thought occurred to me to take one of his forms home, fill it out, and then get a dozen or so copies printed to be handed to any new doctors from here on. To be sure some of the information requested on the form could be very important, mostly to the bookkeeper who sends out the bills and whose duty it is to see that the doctor gets paid, because I don't recall the doctor ever looking at the form. Even though I had an appointment I noticed the waiting room was quite full so the lengthy wait came as no surprise. Making me wait was ill advised on the part of the doctor because the longer I waited the less wholesome was my attitude toward his profession, and out of my steam came a germ of an idea which is about to come to fruition.

It occurred to me after filling out the doctor's questionnaire that he knows quite a bit about me (including items other than just health information) and I know practically nothing about him. This guy came recommended by a friend of my neighbor's cousin who knows less about the medical profession than I do about the theory of relativity. Or worse yet, this doctor was recommended by another doctor who I found out later has never met the doctor he recommended nor has he seen his office. He did admit to me later that he had lunch once with the doctor he had recommended to me. I admired his honesty when I asked him if the guy is any good. His reply was, "I don't know how good he is, but he should be good by virtue of the fact he has performed this operation more times than anybody else I know." Have you noticed that on most of the doctors' forms they want to know on whose recommendation you've come (which translates "to whom do I send the referral fee?"). So here's the idea that resulted from just sitting around a crowded waiting room grinding my teeth.

Why don't I make up a form of my own and let the doctors fill out my form so we'll both know a lot about each other? No doctor with more than two years experience would ever fill out my form under threat of slow torture and dismemberment. You will see why when you study my form. It's all interesting information we'd like to know when selecting a new doctor, but let's

DOCTOR'S QUESTIONNAIRE

NAME:_____DATE: _____
ADDRESS:(BUS) _____PHONE: _____
      (RES) _____PHONE: _____
EDUCATION: SCHOOLS   GRADE POINT AVE.

_____   _____
_____   _____
_____   _____

INTERNSHIP: _____RATING: _____
SPECIALTIES:_____
MALPRACTICE INSURANCE CARRIER _____
AMOUNT: _____
MALPRACTICE SUITS: Please indicate (W=Won, P=Pending L=Lost)
DATE   PLAINTIFF   AMT SOUGHT AMT SETTLED

CONFLICTS OF INTERESTS: (Family investments)
Hospitals   Amount Invested

Pharmacies   Amount Invested

Pharmaceutical Companies   Amount Invested

CONSULTANT AGREEMENTS (Formal and Informal)
DOCTOR   ADDRESS

FEES:MEDICARE AND BLUE CROSS ACCEPTED AS FULL PAYMENT? ❏ YES ❏ NO
HOW MANY PATIENTS DO YOU SEE PER WORK DAY (AVERAGE) _____
HOW MANY PATIENT DEATHS HAVE OCCURRED RESULTING FROM YOUR
OPERATIONS? _____
LIST THEM   OPERATION

HAVE YOU EVER HEARD OF ANY DOCTOR IN THIS LOCALITY LOSING HIS
LICENSE TO PRACTICE? _____IN ANY LOCALITY? _____
NAME HIM OR HER_____
WHAT IS YOUR COUNTRY CLUB? _____
WHAT IS YOUR GOLF HANDICAP?_____
DO YOU DRINK ALCOHOL? _____HOW MANY DRINKS PER DAY? _____
WHAT DRUGS ARE YOU (OR HAVE YOU) TAKEN? _____
EVER BEEN ARRESTED? _____FOR WHAT? _____

have our chuckles and forget it unless some giant like Medicare, Blue Cross or TRW (Thompson Ramo Woolridge) tackles the job, and unfortunately they have no motivation to do so. They are more interested in the cost of the medical care instead of its quality, and rightfully so. They are insurance companies dealing with the financial end of this business and probably are not qualified to judge doctors from a medical standpoint.

This all started as a gag, but the more I thought about it, the idea started to take on a degree of seriousness. TRW has voluminous files on our credit ratings based on information they have gathered from their subscribers. TRW rates our credit as individuals for the benefit of their subscribers. *Consumers Report Magazine* rates various products for the benefit of their subscribers so we can profit from the mistakes of others. Why isn't there some kind of a central file and rating system on doctors that we can consult when selecting a doctor?

The first problem I foresee is that there appears to be a doctors' code that prevents one doctor from speaking unkindly or harshly about another, so where would we get a truly honest report? It's obvious it wouldn't come from The American Medical Association. Medicare and health insurance companies (e.g. Blue Cross, etc.) must have some pretty good files. If they don't have them now, they could generate a huge file very quickly if every claim submitted was accompanied by a performance evaluation of the doctor by the patient. The information on the forms would have to be noted as a matter of personal opinion lest the lawyers get richer than they are now. I had two experiences with one doctor's office that would be worth reporting and are factual and not just a matter of personal opinion.

After having taken a blood panel test, I returned to the doctor's office about two weeks later and asked the nurse how everything came out on the blood panel. She looked at my record and said everything was normal and there was nothing to worry about. A few minutes later when I was alone with the doctor, I asked him how my uric acid test came out on the blood panel. He looked at my records and said the results of the blood panel weren't returned yet from the laboratory. He phoned the laboratory with language that warmed the air demanding results of my blood panel. On another occasion the same doctor gave me a prescription (that I couldn't read) causing my pharmacist to say, "You don't want this stuff, this is what your wife takes." I don't see that doctor any more.

The following was clipped from the *Sacramento Bee* on June 29, 1990:

Questionable Doctors List

BALTIMORE — A consumer advocacy group released Thursday a nationwide compendium that identifies nearly 7,000 medical professionals who have been disciplined by state and federal agencies. The roster, 2 inches thick and titled "6,892 Questionable Doctors," lists actions taken against physicians, dentists, chiropractors and podiatrists in 40 states.

"If your doctor is among the 6,892 on the list, you ought to at least question the quality of his or her care," said Doctor Sidney M. Wolfe, Director of the Public Citizen Research Group, which issued the report.

The consumer group found that while more than 100,000 Americans were killed or injured each year as a result of medical negligence, only 2600 formal disciplinary actions are taken by states annually against doctors, and fewer than one half of one percent of the nation's doctors face any state sanctions each year.

Copies of the guide can be ordered from Public Citizen Health Research Group, Department QD, 2000 P St. N.W., Washington DC 20036.

A radio report of this item revealed that about half of the states in the United States refused to disclose the names of those doctors disciplined or even how many. By reprinting this article I'm not implying that the whole medical profession is sick and in need of help; to the contrary, these are very good statistics (if accurate). Only 2,600 disciplinary actions taken for 100,000 Americans killed or injured appears very suspicious and suggests a well-engineered cover up. The problem is that the names of the doctors disciplined are withheld from the patients.

This field of medical administration will soon progress, in the not too distant future, to a point where we can subscribe to a health insurance company that will maintain our entire medical record from birth on a single computer floppy disk. The record will be a 100% compilation of every medical experience my body has had during my lifetime and will be printed legibly for all to read. It will include doctors' records, prescribed medicines, operations, hospital stays, dental records, etc. and the cost of each item entered. Then when I go to a new community or need a doctor while away from home, the doctor can, with my permission, tap into my complete medical history. Patterns would become very obvious to the medical mind that would be completely overlooked by the patient, (e.g. patients would be forewarned of slowly deteriorating lung capacity early enough to do something about it).

The marketing and advertising departments of health insurance companies could offer this needed service to attract more new clients at very little cost to them by rating doctors, hospitals, new medicines, etc. If I were choosing a new medical insurance company right now, I certainly would be attracted to the company who kept records and accounts of doctors and hospitals as well as patients. The cost of operating such a medical file could be partially offset by selling accumulated results of new medicines and their side effects to pharmaceutical companies and to the Food and Drug Administration to help them with their research activities. These results would in no way compromise the privacy of the individual patient but would allow us to benefit from each other's medical, surgical and administrative experiences. Unfortunately, computers have already reached a point where they are giving us more data than we can assimilate, but fortunately, they can also boil it down in summary form to give us the results without our having to wade through tons of raw materials to draw our own conclusions.

I can't leave this subject without saying I am very pleased with my doctor, optometrist and dentist; it's the elimination process to find them that irks me.

Chapter 7

BALANCED BUDGET

Well here I am again, the voice of futility optimistically shoveling sand against the tide. I want a balanced federal budget, but I'm definitely in the minority and can mathematically prove it. Why have we had an unbalanced budget for so many years? The answer is very simple. Because the majority of all the people in the United States (which includes those who don't vote) permit the government to continue deficit spending our nation into further debt, and here is my proof.

At least 51 percent of our senators have voted in favor of every budget that has exceeded the government's income. More than one half of all the House of Representatives has voted for every budget that was greater than our nation can afford. The President approved all those budgets which exceeded our federal income. Yet the majority of all voters in the United States voted for the President, the senators and the representatives who in turn voted to overspend our income. These are the undeniable facts. And that, my children, is why we do not have a balanced budget. The majority want it this way, and that's the way it's going to be until we change it. Those who didn't bother to vote have silently endorsed all this spending or they would have been voting all along if they had objected. Unfortunately, the non-voting group is the real silent majority. In a democracy it's not majority rule as we have been taught, it's the majority of those who vote that rule. Therefore it should not be a surprise to anybody that our nation is going further into debt every minute. There is another possible cause for this deplorable situation — ignorance!

We have now defined our problem, which is to educate the ignorant, stimulate the lethargic and reverse the thinking of those who have already made up their minds that "deficit spending ain't all that bad." I feel a very warm kinship to Don Quixote right now.

For the benefit of those who don't know what we are talking about, deficit spending is a procedure whereby our government spends more money than it has and goes deep into debt by borrowing money from some people in order to pay back to some other people, with interest, the money they had borrowed earlier. If this were sound financial thinking, we should just give the government a huge credit card, eliminate all taxes completely, and just borrow. Those of us who have credit cards know there is a limit to this type of financial maneuvering, but apparently the government is oblivious to this reality. It is doubtful that even FDR (President Franklin Delano Roosevelt) ever dreamed things could get this far out of hand when he began this deficit spending trend to start the flow of money during the Great Depression of the early thirties. It is OK to get temporarily in debt to finance the recovery of a great depression or World

War II, but it is shear stupidity to continue the debt indefinitely paying billions of dollars annually in interest while postponing the inevitable repayment to the next generation and so on. The interest on the national debt today is far greater than the entire national budget was several years ago. The latest figures show that it requires all the income taxes collected west of the Mississippi to pay the interest on the national debt. What will be the situation at the turn of the century?

Tennessee Ernie Ford once told a story worth repeating now showing us how to start attacking a problem of this nature. A farmer loaned his best mule to his neighbor farmer with the understanding that the mule must be treated with the utmost kindness and gentleness in order to get him to work. The neighbor farmer hitched up the mule to his plow. He spoke softly and then pleaded with the mule to move but without results. An appeal for help brought the mule's owner, who went over to the mule, picked up a fence post, and cracked the mule a severe blow between the eyes, which staggered him. Then he softly said "giddyup" and the mule obeyed. "You said to treat him with gentleness and kindness if I wanted to get any work out of him" the neighbor farmer said to the mule's owner. The mule's owner replied, "Yeah, but ya gotta get his attention first."

This problem of deficit spending is twofold. First, the congress deliberately plans on spending more than the national income by setting a budget greater than our estimated income. Second, the bureaucrats don't stay within the budget that has been set for them. Our problem is to determine whose attention we should get first. Politicians buy their votes with their pork barrel tactics, feeling they would be voted out of office if they didn't support those programs that benefited their constituents more than the nation.

Over the years I have attended many organizational meetings that always began with the flag salute, the invocation and singing the *Star Spangled Banner*, *God Bless America* or *America the Beautiful*. These were followed by a few announcements and the treasurer's report. It might be a good idea for Congress to begin each day's session in a similar manner but shorten the invocation a little and use that time for a treasurer's report, more appropriately call the DEFICIT REPORT. Prayer hasn't seemed to have done the budget much good in the past, so let's try the squeaky wheel approach. The Deficit Report should place a strong emphasis on the good or damage done to the national debt by the budget deficit in their last session. The announcements would be taped playbacks of campaign rhetoric such as Bush's "Read My Lips" speech and the other forgotten campaign promises of our congressmen. This would be a very well spent 15 minutes or so, if the congressmen were awake!

Before the vote on *every* bill involving the expenditure of government funds, an updated DEFICIT REPORT should be repeated. Please don't take this suggestion lightly. The DEFICIT REPORT does not have to be very elaborate, just a simple report such as the following should do the job:

Today's (Month, Day & Year) DEFICIT REPORT is as follows:

National debt (how much we owe)	$3,023,000,000,000
This year's income	Not known
Annual budget (our annual income)	$231,000,000,000
Annual expenditures (how much we've spent)	(Who's keeping track?)
Interest on national debt this year	$254,850,000,000

Interest on national debt (daily)	$698,219,100
National debt change (+ or -) last session	(Figure's unavailable)

NUFF SAID?

A printed copy of this report should be placed on every congressmen's desk each morning as regular as a morning newspaper. If the same simple box score report were printed on the front page of all our major daily newspapers, it would probably get and keep the attention of many voters. Let's give it a try. Suggest it to the editor of your daily paper. Something good might happen.

On June 29, 1990, Paul Harvey reported that our Congress sees our budget deficit as such a serious problem that they are considering a cut in Social Security benefits, and in the same day, they discussed increasing our foreign aid by $13,000,000,000. I guess the message to our elderly is "when retiring, go to a foreign country where your Social Security money is going." This doesn't seem like a very good budget fix to me. Even Congress should be able to come up with a better solution than this one. I always thought that a Congressman's first loyalty was supposed to be to his employer — the American Public. Don't forget congressmen are your employees.

Congress in its diplomatic timidity puts together a budget that doesn't reduce or eliminate any favorite programs of their buddies so naturally the budget never goes down. Nobody wants to take the heat for scrapping somebody else's favorite program. The President is always on the spot because our current law offers him only two budget options, which are "take it" or "leave it." Congress has really overlooked a golden opportunity by not giving the President "line item veto" privileges enjoyed by the majority of the governors in the nation. If the President had his line item veto, Congress could put him on the spot as the fall guy for reducing or dropping somebody's favorite program.

The line item veto would be a good place to start our campaign for sensible government. This is a good first step, but it will take a lot more than a single step to solve this problem so let's look further.

The problem is how to make up a federal budget that will get us out of debt. First we'll estimate our income for the year so we'll know the maximum amount of money we have to spend. Then subtract 10% to start paying our past due bills (debt). Now we know how much money we can budget to operate the federal government. If one item is increased, then ALL other items must take a prorated reduction. This is when we find out if we have any real statesmen in Congress.

If this procedure were law, just think of the economy of having no national debt. Hundreds of BILLIONS of dollars previously spent on interest payments could be saved or spent on something really worthwhile that would benefit all mankind (e.g. research on a hydrocarbon fuel substitute or medical research). It all starts with some pretty loose laws that control (or don't control) the conduct of Congress. Since Congress and our federal bureaucrats have repeatedly acted like children in a toy store with an unlimited credit card, it's time to put some credit restrictions on them, but first let's "get their attention." I worked for a major corporation once that fell temporarily on hard times. Expenses exceeded income and yet all the employees were apparently necessary to get the work done. Everybody received a 10% cut in salary, which got their attention immediately. The salary reduction had a twofold effect. The work force was voluntarily reduced somewhat and those remaining were stimulated. Increased productivity quickly proved all those employees weren't really necessary to accomplish the work. With higher productivity and the economies of a reduced work force, promotions and pay raises soon followed. The president of the company once told a group of his managers, "If you can eliminate your own job or department, tell me how because I have a better job waiting for you." Do you recall the reduction of toll takers at the Golden Gate Bridge related in the Introduction? We need this kind of thinking in the federal government.

A 10 % cut in salary of our bureaucrats would be a good step number two, starting with Congress. The financial loss wouldn't hurt very many of them, but the humiliation would "get their attention."

Let's divide this problem into two problems: Our elected officials in Congress, and the White House and the bureaucrats. The voters must either take the blame for electing politicians who are totally incompetent in business matters or who really know what they are doing. Even when one politician is defeated, which is a rare occasion, he is replaced by another of the same ilk and the problem continues. Maybe some new laws to protect us from these repeated over-spenders would get their attention. An example is a constitutional amendment prohibiting the Congress from borrowing money without a 90% approval vote of each house of Congress and the President. When the money runs out before the end of the fiscal year, Congress and many bureaucrats wouldn't get paid. We should be able to elect at least 10% of our politicians to keep the other 90% in line. Probably it would be a good idea if the law prohibited any congressman from governmental employment of any kind for a period of five years after he served a term in a Congress that exceeded its budget. This automatic lame duck provision would benefit us in two ways. It would have a sobering influence on the daily activity of our elected officials and, if that failed, it would assure us that we wouldn't have the same incompetent officials for another term. These ideas require a little refinement, but I think you get the idea and I'm sure our elected officials would get the point in a hurry.

The second problem is our bureaucrats. Jerry Brown once said his first real shock when taking office as Governor of California was finding out he only had the power to fire six state employees, and those were his own office staff and a chauffeur! It is almost impossible to fire a civil servant. I don't like that term civil servant because servants are usually people that WORK for you.

Government pensions are another huge expense which should be analyzed. I hear that Senator Alan Cranston of California, of Lincoln Savings and Loan fame, is still on the government payroll while drawing six government pensions. Is this right? Why should government employees receive better pension benefits than the taxpayers who support them?

Our postal system is about as exposed as any governmental department, so look it over closely. How does it compare to United Parcel Service, Federal Express, etc.? Free enterprise seems to be doing a much better job for less money and making a profit at it while paying taxes. The reasons for this difference don't really matter. What I'm really saying is why try to straighten out the Post Office Dept. when it would be more practical to replace it by dividing up the nation into districts, areas, localities, cities, counties etc. and putting the job of mail carrying out for contracts of five or ten year's duration? There is a term called GOCO used in the Department of Defense. It is an acronym for Government Owned Contractor Operated. I believe the Army Tank Plant in Detroit is run this way. Why can't the Post Office and many other government civil service operations be handled the same way? It's worth looking into.

One of the beautiful things about free enterprise is that the incompetent, the inefficient and the inept ultimately fail and disappear. They really don't disappear — they end up on welfare or working for the government.

Another major reason for our budget imbalance is huge subsidies which fall into three categories. Two of these categories are so well hidden we can't put our finger on them to analyze how much they really cost us.

The first subsidy is out in the open when we write a check and give money to wheat farmers, tobacco farmers, foreign counties, thousands of grants, etc. Our government buys wheat from our farmers and then sells it to Russia for less than they paid for it. I forget, are we subsidizing our farmers or Russia? We know how much this is costing us because we write checks that can be totalled, although I don't recall any government report listing all the subsidies with a price tag on each.

The second subsidy is highlighted in Chapter I, Income Taxes. This subsidy amounts to all the taxes that are not collected from special interest groups. Let's face it, the way the law is currently written, everyone in the United States is in several special interest groups. We subsidize interest payments, medical bills, large families, charities, religions, business losses, etc. with tax deductions. Keep in mind that the issue in this case isn't which subsidies are good or bad, the issue is whether to expose them with their price tag so they can be analyzed. Get the IRS out of the subsidy business and save some money. If you skipped

Chapter 1, I urge you to go back and read it or maybe even re-read it.

The third huge subsidy is the services we give away. It sounds ridiculous to say that we are subsidizing two of the wealthiest nations in the world, Germany and Japan. A very substantial portion of most nations' budgets goes to their military department except for Japan and Germany. These two nations are getting a free ride in this department at our expense. For obvious reasons, after World War II it seemed like a good idea to prevent them from again becoming a threat to world peace. By denying them a significant military force we (the Allies) took on the responsibility of being their protectorate. This allowed each of them a tremendous tax economy so they could concentrate on commerce, which they have done admirably well and prospered. Being their protectorate isn't necessarily a bad idea, but they should pay for this service instead of buying up the world with the money we have saved them. This brings up the subject of reciprocal trade, which might be considered another subsidy. Japan's economy is booming from the money we spend on their goods, while they deny us the opportunity to compete in their markets. Who is it that permits this debacle to continue? It isn't Japan.

The next time you vote for a senator, representative or president analyze his platform with regard to deficit spending and demand from him (or her) his plan to eliminate the national debt. Don't accept generalities but a definite plan and time schedule for accomplishing complete solvency. It is unfortunate that our ballots don't permit the option of "NONE OF THE ABOVE" so we can reject them all until somebody presents a definite detailed financial get well plan.

There are only two ways to balance the budget and eventually eliminate the national debt. Either take in more money or spend less money. Raising taxes should be a last resort, and then only after we have closely analyzed our spending. By way of summary, here are some possibilities to reduce spending which are not listed in order of priority. These are raw ideas which will require serious thought and refinement before being put into practice. Feel free to expand the list.

- Cut the government payroll 5 or 10%.

- Let Japan and Germany pay us (and the other Allies) for their national defense.

- Stop the one-way flow of commerce with reciprocal laws. If we can't sell in their market, then the same applies here. This should result in a free market world wide.

- Analyze and reduce subsidies after they are exposed. If necessary they should be reduced 10% across the board. Instead of reducing the value of the dollar by over-spending, let's reduce the number of dollars spent.

- Government pensions should start 65 years of age.

- Give the President "line item veto" to help him cut spending.

- Get the IRS out of the subsidy business, which should result in a payroll saving of at least three billion dollars.

- Disqualify any President, Senator or Representative who supports an unbalanced budget from further government employment for five years.

I have little confidence in our government being able to change it's habits without the proper stimulation. If you wish to join my campaign for a balanced budget, let me suggest the following sample letter be sent to every successful politician after his election.

Senator_____,
Senate Office Bldg.
Washington, D.C. 20510

Dear Senator _____,

You are to be congratulated on your successful campaign for the office of Senator, and I wish you the best of luck during your term of office. You have my enthusiastic support.

During your campaign, you expressed your views on many subjects so we would know what to expect from you. At this time, it is appropriate that I express my view on a balanced budget and how strongly I feel its necessity, so you will know what to expect from me. This should be your number one priority every year of your term of office.

I want to see a 5% reduction in the national debt this coming year with larger reductions each successive year with savings from lower debt interest payments ALL going to further debt reduction until the nation no longer has a debt.

Should you (and the government) fail in this regard I shall actively and vigorously fight your reelection at the end of your term of office. I expect you will receive many similar letters in this regard in the very near future.

Sincerely,

Chapter 8

RETIREE - CONSULTANTS

Many years ago I worked for a wonderful corporation that might have had one big fault. They were very paternalistic. They might have cared too much about their employees. About five years before an employee was due to retire they would call him into the office to ensure he had at least one hobby if not more. About a year after the employee retired they would look him up to see if he had "Rocking-chair-itis" and was just sitting, rocking and staring into space. Whenever they found a stagnant retiree, they would often try to hire him back as a consultant for a short period of time to solve a company problem and make him feel useful in this world.

I complemented the personnel department for their wonderful attitude and got a reply I didn't expect. Yes, we are interested in our retirees, but they are a wealth of knowledge and experience you couldn't buy any place in the world and it's a shame to see it go to waste. Our policies are extremely beneficial to both

the retiree and the corporation. It's a bilaterally beneficial system.

There are many benefits from hiring retired employees as
consultants. They are hired for a week, month, year or until a
problem is solved. They can be hired as independent contractors with a minimum amount of paperwork, so there are no employee benefits (e.g. insurance, vacation and sick pay, social
security, workman's compensation, etc.) to be concerned with,
just a simple contract and the paper work is done. The price of
their service is negotiable and depends on how busy they are at
the time and many other factors. If the price is high, it is
probably worth it. All the experience you are getting still makes
it a bargain.

The other great advantage is their availability. If the job
doesn't interfere with their fishing, camping or rocking they can
start right now.

There is a famous story of the firm that hired a consultant
for $1000 because of a breakdown on their electronically con-
trolled assembly line. The consultant arrived on the job, walked
around with a quizzical look on his face and humming to himself. After about ten minutes of this, he went over to the electronic panel and banged it once with a solid blow. Everything
started working and the problem was solved in less than fifteen
minutes. He presented them with his bill for $1,000.00 as agreed.
Their reaction was slightly more than horrified. They said,
"$1,000.00 for less than fifteen minutes work is ridiculous and
we won't pay it, unless you give us a breakdown of your bill!"
"Fine," he said, "$5.00 for the bang and $995.00 for knowing
where to bang." It's an old story but it really proves my point.
There is no substitute for experience.

The problem is where to find the right specialist among these retired employees for the job you need done. (Read Chapter 19 for a possible answer.) We need a hiring hall for this extremely knowledgeable and experienced group. The AARP (American Association of Retired Persons) could do a real service to their membership if they would start a consultants hiring hall. They could come up with an expert in just about every field of endeavor that exists (production, chemical, mechanical, marketing, farming, etc. and the list goes on forever).

The first place for a company to look for a consultant is its own list of retired employees. They know your product and your system, and best of all, their wealth of experience can tell you many things that won't work because things that have been tried before and failed are rarely well documented. This should be your first choice.

I hope somebody with the AARP reads this and investigates the idea. There are many very knowledgeable, experienced and bored retirees running around, and there many companies with problems who need consultants. The problem is that there is no way for them to find each other. Here is a chance for the AARP to perform a real service and make a little income at the same time.

Chapter 9

SUNSET LAWS

In ancient Egypt a couple of thousand years ago, a Pharaoh summoned his wise men and asked them to prepare a statement that would always be true under all conditions. The wise men worked for days discarding statement after statement trying to compose the perfect statement. Finally they sent word to the Pharaoh that they had the statement. The statement they gave to the Pharaoh was "And This Too Shall Come To Pass."

There is little point in planning for obsolescence, because it will get here all by itself totally unassisted. Some things will be obsolete before others, like this book. Fortunately laws are not like Longfellow's "One Horse Shay" that was so perfectly engineered and constructed that every part broke simultaneously after 100 years and a day. In a highly technical industry, where I once worked, technology advanced daily, and we considered the production of a single article a "production run." Some chapters of this book will be obsolete before the book is finished.

The same is true of our laws. They are usually referred to as blue laws.

About twenty years ago there was still a law on the books in Los Angeles that made it illegal to shoot jack rabbits from a moving street car with a revolver. There was no mention of a rifle or a stopped street car. About that time Philadelphia had a law on the books against firing a cannon on the main streets of the city after sun down. It apparently was okay to fire it during the day. These examples are extremely obvious, whereas laws less ancient are still on their way to becoming obsolete. Even the Constitution, which is a beautifully written document, has about twenty five amendments to keep it up to date.

Whatever happened to that old ritual called "spring house cleaning"? As children we were required to empty out our closets and drawers to discard obsolete and worn out stuff. It wasn't a pleasant job, but it left us feeling good when the job was done. The really tough parts were sometimes neglected — the basement, attic and garage. If these were ignored long enough, they would eventually reach a saturation point and become intolerable.

California has enacted 14,899 laws since 1981, which averages about 1800 new laws per year. I hope it is only coincidental that California got about 1800 new lawyers last year. What a revolting thought — gain a law, gain a lawyer. At that rate we will have an additional 16,624 more laws by the turn of the century, or another way to look at it is that my 10-year-old grandchildren will see 121,054 laws enacted during the remainder of their lives. Absolutely absurd! With every new law we lose a little more of our freedom and gain a new lawyer. Where will it end?

Maybe it would be a good idea to start every legislative session with a good "spring house cleaning." To assure that the basement, attic and garage aren't ignored, every law should have an automatic expiration date. Laws with an expiration date are called "SUNSET LAWS." Law expiration dates might be exactly one year for new laws, three years for the second review, and ten years for the third and subsequent reviews. These suggested review dates are not meant to precluded other reviews as necessary.

Just about every law ever written could be written better after we have had a little experience with the law the way it was originally written. In revising old laws, it should be kept in mind that the ambiguity and complexity of the law increases by the square of the number of words written. A good example is our income tax law that has increased from about seventeen pages to about fifty volumes after many revisions, and it certainly can't be described as the epitome of clarity today. Tests have shown that even those who are paid to administer the income tax law will give you a wrong answer over 40% of the time when consulted for help. At this rate, with a few more revisions, nobody will understand any portion of the law. Let's not forget "KISS" in the introduction to this book. If passing the law was a mistake in the first place, it would automatically disappear if not reviewed and re-passed by the legislature. Some laws should be allowed to die, while others should be refined to fit the current situation and political thinking.

The expiration dates would automatically be staggered depending on the date the law was originally written or last reviewed, except for that avalanche of laws numbering in the hundreds that were passed on the last day that the legislature met.

Almost all laws can probably be polished a bit (hopefully simplified) several years after they have been written. What was clear to the lawmakers at the time the law was written is usually discovered to be not so clear to others at a later date. Here is where that old cliché comes in — "we're going to keep doing this until we get it right."

Hopefully the sunset law concept would not become a "Pandora's Box" and create change for the sake of change. There was once a wonderful slogan in three foot high letters on the wall in front of the engineering staff at Piasecki Helicopter plant which read "IF IT IS NOT NECESSARY TO CHANGE, IT IS NECESSARY NOT TO CHANGE." A similar sign might be a good idea in our legislature.

Any law establishing sunset laws should also have a provision requiring revisions to an old law *must* contain fewer words than the original law. This provision will cause our law makers to choke!

This is another case of "you have to take the bad with the good." While our laws would be getting better (or hopefully expiring or being eliminated) an added burden would be placed on our society to keep informed of all these changes. It's hard enough now to keep current, and it could become intolerable. Along with the bad there is another side effect that has pleasant consequences. Our law makers would be so busy trying to straighten out their past mistakes, they would be too busy to make many new mistakes.

Chapter 10

SOCIAL SECURITY

A few generations back, retirement was experienced by relatively few people. It required investing money in property and successful business ventures. The safest investment was postal savings which paid about 2% interest, so it took a lot of savings to produce a little bread in the future. Retirement for wage earners was very different. It usually meant moving in with your kids and grandchildren, or vice versa they moved in with you to keep up the family homestead and for you to baby sit the grandchildren. It meant living off the family. Rocking chairs were an essential piece of equipment for the retired. Saving for your old age retirement is a good idea, but it went against the grain of the Keynesian economists who said it took too much money out of the economy.

In the great depression of the early thirties, the Roosevelt administration started our Social Security System primarily to support the Keynesian theories. This was not an original idea.

Chile began their Social Security System in 1924.

Handing over your savings to our government is comparable to asking an alcoholic to guard your liquor cabinet. Saving is a wonderful idea and should be mandatory for those who lack the good judgement to do it voluntarily. Saving should be mandatory for everybody but sending your savings to Washington should be optional. Forcing us to hand over our money to the "spendaholics" in Washington doesn't support my idea of a prudent investment. We should be provided the option of investing our money in either the government or in other approved institutions, or some combination of both.

The following quotations are from Warren T. Brookes, a syndicated economist based in Washington D. C., who supports this concept. We can learn a great deal from studying other countries' successes and failures as well as our own.

Warren T. Brookes — *San Francisco Chronicle,* June 27, 1989 —

The main reason that the Roosevelt administration launched the Social Security system was the argument of Keynesian economists that Americans were "saving too much." The Social Security system was a deliberate attempt to take money from the savers and put it in the hands of the consumers and reduce saving for retirement.

It worked only too well. It is no accident that as total taxes for federal social insurance, including Medicare, have soared three percent points from 6.4 percent of personal income in 1970 to 9.5 percent in 1988, personal savings have fallen more than 3 points — from 6.9 percent to last year's dismal 3.5 percent. In short we have nationalized a major portion of our savings through the Social Security system.

In 1980 Chile's economy was in bad shape and their social security system was nearly bankrupt with the government paying 28 percent of the benefits out of general revenues in spite of total payroll taxes amounting to 36 percent of wages. (The figure is 14 percent in the U. S.)

In 1980 Jose Pinera, minister of Labor and Social Welfare, offered workers the freedom to leave the Social Security System — carrying with them a government bond covering all their accumulated benefits — and join a private system, where their individual accounts would be managed by their choice of 12 investment companies specifically chartered and regulated by the government.

The investment target of the plan is to give the worker 70 percent of his final five years of pay as compared with 45 percent in the U.S. system.

When 90 percent of the workers elected that alternative, Chile generated a massive new pool of investment capital, which has fueled what is now the strongest economy in Latin America. Large in-flows of foreign capital rushed to get in on its 7 percent GNP and this has cut its external debt by 37 percent since 1984.

These figures are pretty close to the study performed several years ago that showed a U.S. worker retiring today, having been in our Social Security plan from its inception, would be receiving 192 percent of today's Social Security benefits if his savings had been invested in a private plan.

Where does our Social Security money go after we send it to Washington? Does it stay in the economy some way, invested, or just go away? Where do the Japanese get the money to buy up most of our major cities, businesses and banks? Does it come from their government through taxes or from the financial institutions full of savings? I have heard the Japanese have one the highest rates of savings of any country in the world.

Our students and educational system are slipping downhill rapidly when compared to foreign countries, and the educational and intelligence level of our Washington bureaucrats is leading the downhill slippage race. Are we too proud and egotistical to admit somebody else's system is better than ours?

Let's give some serious consideration to copying the Social Security System of Chile where the workers have the option of staying with the federal government or going with a private system or maybe some combination of both. What have we to lose?

Chapter 11

UNITED NATIONS

Not very long ago, practically yesterday by geological time, the world was so huge that what people did on one side of the world didn't in any way effect the people on the other side of the world. As a matter of fact, as recently as five hundred years ago the people on one side of the world didn't even know there was another side of the world with people living there. Small wars that occurred here and there were confined to the immediate locality and not too troublesome to the rest of the world. Then came World War I, which involved a large portion of the world. It was a great lesson to be learned, but it wasn't learned.

Then came World War II that involved just about everybody in the world from the center of large cities to the back hills of Borneo. We learned much about mass destruction, and then came the atomic bomb. Now we had a really gigantic world-wide problem, and many people decided this was the time to take serious action to see that it would never happen again. The proposed corrective effort must include the support and involvement of the whole world in order to be effective.

When Eleanor Roosevelt, Harold Stassen and many others got together with representatives from other nations in San Francisco on April 25, 1945 to create the charter for the United Nations, it was believed to be the answer to world peace. The idea was a noble one, but it lost a lot in the execution. The operating rules set up resembled a passenger train with every passenger having a brake handle that could stop the train at any time or even prevent it from leaving the station. It's almost impossible to make any forward progress under these conditions.

The United Nations has been a colossal failure. It didn't even work when only one nation had the atom bomb and the United States has no monopoly on brains, human energy, drive, resources and ambition, so it was only a matter of time before other nations would have a nuclear arsenal. And it is still only a matter of time before every nation on the earth can have nuclear capacity if it so wishes. Let's start calling them nuclear bombs to include the hydrogen bomb.

Now with many nations having nuclear bombs, the original train illustration referring to the UN charter has changed to a large pressurized cabin on a passenger airplane with five hundred passengers plus their juvenile children, each having a hand grenade capable of destroying the plane (or the world in this case). One ignorant or deranged nut can do it deliberately or accidentally. Although there was a serious need for a peace organization in 1946 the need is a thousand times greater today and getting more critical every minute. It is inevitable and won't be long before rulers like Hitler, Mussolini, Tojo, Moammar Khadafy, Ayatollah Ruhollah Khomeini, Fidel Castro, Idi Amin, Yasir Arafat, and every terrorist organization in the world will eventually have nuclear bomb capabilities. This is not merely conjecture, it is inevitable, and plans must be made to cope with the situation when it occurs. Not if, but when. The attack on Pearl Harbor was a mere childish prank compared to the possibility of a surprise nuclear attack.

In spite of all these gloom and doom thoughts there is a small bright side. If Afghanistan had had a few good nuclear bombs about ten years ago, along with the capability to deliver them, the Russian army would have stayed home. The same thing could be said of all aggressive armies.

We have taken the UN a little too lightly, feeling it was harmless because it was doing nothing. The UN is to the world what phoney medicine is to a cancer patient. The phoney medicine, although harmless, is preventing the patient from getting the real help he needs. The UN Charter was put together by some very idealistic people who naïvely believed the world would become very idealistic also. It will never be successful as long as part of the world is playing hard ball and the remainder is playing softball.

The fundamental purpose of the UN was to put a stop to war. Can you name a war the UN has prevented or stopped? When the UN created the state of Israel (rightly or wrongly) it took on an obligation to see it through. When the UN makes a mistake, how is it corrected? The Security Council of the UN Charter has provisions whereby a single nation acting alone can stop any constructive effort of the rest by the world.

It is difficult to find anything nice to say about the UN. Here are a few of its missed opportunities:

What has it done about:

1. international drugs?
2. worldwide state-sponsored terrorism and kidnapping?
3. population explosion?
4. AIDS research?
5. poison gas manufacturing and use?
6. airplane hijacking?
7. famine relief in Ethiopia?
8. world ecology?
9. rain forests?
10. oceans?
11. whales?
12. dolphins?
13. ozone holes?
14. the green house effect?
15. etc.

The UN has become the international spy headquarters with master spies running around with diplomatic immunity. If over night a spy detector could be invented and used at the UN like metal detectors are used at airports, the UN Headquarters building would be an empty shell the next day.

I can see a bunch of UN supporters warming up the tar for me while their buddies are gathering the feathers. They can make a real case out of the wonderful things the UN has done, but which of the above problems have they solved?

What are our alternatives?

1. Dissolve the UN? We can't do this alone.

2. Revise the charter to make it an effective organization? We can't do this alone either.

3. Close our eyes and let it remain a token peace organization doing nothing good or bad? We're already doing that. Or,

4. Force the UN to live up to its original principles by changing its charter.

When a catastrophic event contrary to international law occurs, the United States should demand that the UN take positive and decisive steps to correct the situation immediately and punish those nations who have broken the law. The demand should carry with it an nonnegotiable condition that if corrective action is not taken in a very short prescribed length of time, then the United States will withdraw from the UN, break off relations with the UN, and tell the UN to relocate someplace outside the United States. If such decisive action were taken, what would it mean to the United States? It would mean we would have to go it alone. Is that any different than what we are doing now? Do we really need an ineffective UN, or does the UN need us more?

The events that should bring about these strong actions would be comparable to Iran taking hostage United States diplomats, taking private citizens hostage, the invasion of Pakistan by Russia, the invasion of any country by another, etc. When a nation attempts to censor the world's reading material by threatening the lives of authors and publishers in other countries, the UN should demand an immediate apology and retraction of the threats or immediate expulsion from the UN with strong sanctions if those threatened are ever harmed in any way.

My personal feelings are that we should move the UN to a desert island where it should have been placed in the first place. Then as a nation, we should sit by patiently until the day when something so drastic happens that suddenly the U.S., the Soviet Block, the EC, NATO, China, Japan, India and a flock of other nations all decide to put the world's interests above their own. On that day we will create an effective peace organization. Hope it's not too late then!

This new peace organization doesn't have to be "one worldism" to be successful. Each nation can still maintain its individuality, whether it is a monarchy, democracy, communistic, or dictatorship makes no difference to the remainder of the world as long as world conquest, slavery, or violation of human rights are not part of its doctrine. The master peace organization would only interfere in matters where the rights of another nation or the world are involved.

How much time do we have before it is too late?

SEPTEMBER 8, 1990

UPDATE 1990

With all the events of the last few weeks in the Persian Gulf, it seemed appropriate to review this chapter the very last minute before going to the printers. After rereading this chapter, I found my opinion of the UN is unchanged, however, I did feel it necessary to expand as follows:

Publishing this book has been a trial because very important new opinions are being formed or reinforced daily. Since the original writing of this chapter, Iraq has invaded and captured Kuwait which required about five hours which exacerbates my original opinion on the subject.

If the UN is ever to succeed, it must be unselfishly supported by the world's wealthiest and most powerful nations. Japan and Germany need Persian Gulf oil more than almost any other nations. In this regard, I fail to understand our treatment of Japan and Germany. Can you name one Japanese war criminal who was prosecuted after World War II? Since World War II, we have converted both Japan and Germany from two totally defeated nations into two of the world's most prosperous nations. And they say crime doesn't pay. Now, while most of the UN is contributing their soldiers, aircraft and ships to stop Iraq's systematic military take over of the world's oil supply, Japan's contribution is business as usual by sending new cars and supplies to Iraq. Business as usual means Japan sells their products in everybody's market and keeps foreign commerce out of their own market while the world provides their national defense and protects them. Japan reported an increase of 6% in their export trade in August 1990 while the world (22 nations) with hostages at stake are fighting their battle for them. WHY?

It's not enough to say something must be done. The something must be well defined and agreed by the UN member nations which takes much time and discussion. One of the main problems of the UN is trying to get many nations to agree on a single objective. My wife and I rarely agree 100% which means somebody must give a little (or a lot). Even without a time limit, is it possible to get many nations to agree on anything? With a time limit of a few hours the chances of an agreement diminish to about zero.

I am strongly opposed to war and fighting and as the old story goes I'm willing to fight for peace. However, when I am required to fight I want a clear understanding what it is that I'm fighting for. In the case of Iraq I have seven nonnegotiable objectives plus a couple of very strong recommendations as follows:

Nonnegotiable objectives:

1. Iraq must get out of Kuwait 100%.

2. Iraq must return all gold and other goods taken from Kuwait.

3. Iraq must have a new government of their choice. In other words, they must elect their government with provisions to displace their leaders by simply voting.

4. All poison gas must be destroyed.

5. All poison gas manufacturing facilities must be destroyed.

6. The government of Kuwait must be restored to power unless the citizens of Kuwait want a different government. That means let them vote for their government and a constitution which allows a change of government by vote.

7. All nuclear research facilities in Iraq must be destroyed with iron clad provisions for a perpetual UN inspection system to guarantee that they will never again be created.

Very Strong Recommendations:

1. Saddam Hussein should be tried as a war criminal; however, it is highly unlikely that he could survive the humiliation if the above objectives are achieved.

2. All military action should be initially confined to Iraq. After Iraq is defeated, the Iraqi forces in Kuwait will be relatively helpless. It is important that the people of Iraq suffer the consequences of war rather than the people of Kuwait.

Anything short of these objectives is not worth fighting for. To negotiate a settlement for less would be an insult to our military and would be a major victory for Saddam Hussein and all the other robbers, thieves, kidnappers, terrorists, rapists and international thugs. It would also be a 100% guarantee of many worse crises in the very near future when these international thugs have nuclear weapons. The world (including the people of Iraq) and our military personnel in Saudi Arabia should have a very clearly defined objective of this military action so they will know what we are fighting for. Many of the people of Iraq might even look favorably on these objectives as opposed to the terrible devastation they will receive if Saddam Hussein decides to fight it out. Let's make our objectives known to the world and especially for the morale of our own troops.

Now with regard to the hostages, I strongly suggest (as of today, Sept. 8, 1990) that leaflets be dropped from a ballistic missile over the most densely populated areas in Iraq with the following message:

SADDAM HUSSEIN (WHO HAS MURDERED MANY OF HIS OPPONENTS) HAS DECIDED TO MATCH Y OUR 17,000,000 LIVES IN IRAQ WITH THE 3,000 HOSTAGES HE IS NOW HOLDING. HE HAS TOTAL DISREGARD FOR THE LIVES OF IRAQI WOMEN, MOTHERS, CHILDREN AND BABIES (AS WELL AS THE LIVES OF HIS HOS-TAGES). IF ALL HOSTAGES ARE NOT RELEASED WITHIN THREE DAYS, A SYSTEMATIC BOMBING OF ALL IRAQ CITIES WILL BEGIN AT 8:00 AM ON _____(DATE).

Dropping these leaflets from a ballistic missile should prove to the people of Iraq just how vulnerable they are and that Saddam Hussein has gotten them into very serious trouble with the world. It should also make them realize the war will be fought in their front yard and not in some far off place where they will not be hurt. If the hostages are released, Hussein's credibility would be virtually destroyed and we'd probably be dealing with a more sane government.

This must not be an idle threat because there is no alterna-tive except to surrender the world piece by piece to all thugs who hold hostages. If you have a better alternative, come up with it quickly.

For all those pacifists who feel this is a cruel plan the following two questions need answering, immediately:

1. How long will it be before Hussein has nuclear bombs? Two years, four years, and five years are the three estimates I have heard from the experts.

2. Do you think a man who has systematically murdered his opponents, including the husband of the woman he wanted, and who has used poison gas on his enemies and his own people, would hesitate to use atomic weapons if he had them now?

These are my minimum demands for my support. Do you think the UN would go along with these objectives? If they did, it would require a minimum of several weeks or months of debates and speeches, and after they did agree on what should be done, would they each commit men, military force and financial support to carry out the plan? Although it is necessary to to have finite stated objectives, our united front against Hussein would be seriously weakened. This is a chance we must take. Only a true war monger or masochist would fight a war without known objectives. In school I got an "A" in naivete and idealistic thinking and then came the real world.

If the UN could not agree on its objectives, would we be willing to fight this battle alone? Isn't this just about where we are now? Russia is correct: this should be a UN action and why isn't it? When this fracas is over who will accept the surrender of Iraq? Would it be the US, Britain, France, Saudi Arabia, the UN or who? If it is not the US, how can we be assured that our objectives will be met if they are not agreed to before the hostilities start? Naturally Hussein will attempt to make peace with each country separately like he is attempting with Iran.

Chapter 12

VICE PRESIDENT

During our county's brief history, we have had forty Vice Presidents of which only nine have been called upon to perform their primary function, which is to replace the president due to his temporary inability to perform his job or, if necessary, complete his term of office. The Vice President may replace the President at any moment so naturally we require that our Vice Presidents be of presidential calibre and be ready to instantly take over the President's job if for any reason the President is incapacitated. This means the Vice President must have drive, ambition, energy, personality, leadership qualities, acumen, and be politically astute enough to have a record of accomplishments. He (or she) must have another quality which is completely contrary to all other qualifications. He must be willing to play second fiddle to the president, play a lot of golf, shake many hands, smile a lot, publicly agree with the President (or bite his lip and smile), attend state funerals, and most of all to not upstage the President at any time. He will have no significant duties or responsibilities (except for those special assignments doled out by the President) and will accomplish nothing on his own. This "accomplish nothing on his own" is not quite as true during the last few presidencies as it was in our early history.

To be prepared to jump in at any time, he should be constantly briefed on all issues, however this has not been the practice in the past. When Franklin Roosevelt died during World War II, Harry Truman had to be briefed on the Manhattan Project (the atom bomb). The Vice President was not consulted on even the most crucial problems of the nation.

The Vice President of the United States may technically be the number two man, but the unfortunate person holding this job has absolutely no power except when the Senate vote is evenly divided and a tie breaker is required. Then they allow the VP to open his mouth and vote. When assessing political influence in Washington D.C., the very scientific P.P.P. (Power & Popularity Poll consisting of my barber and me) which agrees with one of the TV networks rates the President first, Ted Koppel second, then David Brinkley and Walter Cronkite, and finally we get down to the politicians. The VP didn't even make the list. Sam Donaldson rates a list all his own. 'Nuff said.

Since only about twenty percent of our Vice Presidents have ever replaced their Presidents, this job doesn't appear to be very attractive for a truly ambitious and talented politician. It is interesting to note that of the nine Vice Presidents who have replaced their Presidents, only four have been reelected after finishing their President's incomplete term.

How much does it cost us to have the Vice President sitting around?

Salary ....$_____

Housing ....$_____

Allowances ....$_____

Cars ....$_____

Transportation..........................$_____

Office ....$_____

Staff..$_____

Secret Service:

        salaries

        offices

        housing

        travel

        meals

        special equipment

        etc.

            Total......................$ _____

            Grand total ....$ _____

My guess is about $25,000,000 per year or $100,000,000 for a four year term.

I don't know the total costs for a retired Vice President but a retired President doesn't come cheap. Here are the costs for retiring Ronald and Nancy Reagan for the remainder of their lives.

1. Around-the-clock Secret Service protection.

2. $300,000 per year office allowance.

3. Pension $99,500 per year for life (soon to be $155,000).

4. Lifetime Secret Service for Nancy Reagan.

5. Penthouse office suite in Century City, California.

6. Townhouse in Washington D.C.

7. Around-the-clock Secret Service protection for his new home in Bel-Air, California.

8. Around-the-clock Secret Service protection for his 688 acre ranch in Santa Barbara, California.

9. Process and ship his papers to California (estimated to cost $500,000).

10. $1,300,000 allowance for storage of the presidential papers.

Not bad for a job that only pays about six times the poverty level. It might cost less to keep them in office the rest of their lives. Just think of it, in addition to Ronald and Nancy Reagan, we have Jimmy and Rosalynn Carter, Gerald and Betty Ford, and Richard and Pat Nixon (plus all their Vice Presidents and wives) all on the payroll as long as they live.

The Constitution provides for a line of succession to the office of the presidency when the President (or his replacement) is incapacitated for any reason.

Order of Presidential Succession

1. Vice President	2. Speaker of the House
3. President pro Tempore	4. Sec. of State
5. Sec. of the Treasury	6. Sec. of Defense
7. Attorney General	8. Sec. of the Interior

9. Sec. of Agriculture	10. Sec. of Commerce
11. Sec. of Labor	12. Sec. of Health & Human Services
13. Sec. of Housing & Human Development	14. Sec. of Transportation
15. Sec. of the of Energy	16. Sec. of Education

Note: All sixteen are appointed officials except the speaker of the House and the president pro tempore of the Senate.

The office of the Vice President of the United States is not truly an elected office for it is merely a small part of a packaged deal. It seems a little inconsistent in a democracy that we are not permitted to vote for such a high office.

How much does the selection of a vice-presidential candidate influence the outcome of a presidential election? In my opinion the only benefits derived from selecting a vice presidential candidate are to give the press a field day speculating who it will be, and then another field day criticizing the selection after it is announced. How much would history have been changed if we had never had the office of Vice President? Not Much! Study the following list of our Vice Presidents and make your own determination.

We don't have "vice senators" nor "vice representatives" sitting around playing the waiting game so why have a Vice President. At least in California we are permitted to vote for our number-two state politician, our lieutenant governor, which is actually more senseless than voting the for the Vice President. A few years back, California elected a democratic governor and a republican lieutenant governor who refused to speak to each other. There was a humorous side to this idiocy. The governor seldom left the state because he would have had to reverse everything his lieutenant governor had done while he was away, and the lieutenant governor had announced several things he would do the next time the governor left the state. This didn't win any smart prizes for California voters.

I personally would not feel cheated if the order of presidential succession were shortened from sixteen officers down to fifteen. So let's save a few hundred million dollars by eliminating the job and turn over the only official vice-presidential duty of President of the Senate to the President Pro Tempore of the Senate (who incidentally is already on our payroll and was elected by his constituency and his peers in the Senate).

The only requirement to make this significant change is a constitutional amendment that amends a few articles (e.g. Art. 1 Sec. 3; Article II, Section I and Amendment XX) in the Constitution. Just a few words changed and voilá, a few hundred million dollars saved. If we eliminate the office of the Vice President from the presidential line of succession, we should make the provision that the President's replacement shall be of the same political party as the President, whether the replacement is the speaker of the House, the majority leader or minority leader of the House.

Here are the nine Vice Presidents who have succeeded their President and have served the remainder of his term of office:

President	Vice President
1. William H. Harrison	John Tyler
2. Zachary Taylor	Millard Fillmore
3. Abraham Lincoln	Andrew Johnson

4. James Garfield   Chester Arthur

5. William McKinley   Theodore Roosevelt

6. Warren G. Harding   Calvin Coolidge

7. Franklin D. Roosevelt   Harry S. Truman

8. John F. Kennedy   Lyndon B. Johnson

9. Richard M. Nixon   Gerald Ford (appointed)

The following is a list of our past Vice Presidents who sat around on the government payroll doing nothing and never became President either by succession or election at a later date:

Arron Burr	George Clinton
Gerry Elbridge	Daniel Tompkins
John Calhoun	Richard Johnson
George Dallas	William King
John Breckinridge	Hannibal Hamlin
Schuyler Colfax	Henry Wilson
William Wheeler	Thomas Hendricks
Levi Morton	Adlai Stevenson
Garret Hobart	Charles Fairbanks
James Sherman	Thomas Marshall
Charles Dawes	Charles Curtis
John Garner	Henry Wallace
Alben Barkley	Hubert Humphrey
Spiro T. Agnew	Walter F. Mondale
Dan Quayle	

What a terrible waste of talent and money!

Chapter 13

FEDERAL SAVINGS & LOAN INSURANCE CORPORATION

I have lain awake many nights dreaming up "get-rich schemes" and every idea I have come up with so far has had gaping holes of uncertainty in it or was illegal. The best scheme of all was the one where I would go to Las Vegas and gamble recklessly with borrowed money, keep all the winnings, and get somebody else to pay for all the losses. I didn't think this was a very promising idea because where would I find a patsy that dumb? I should have given the idea more thought and research and maybe I would have eventually stumbled across the Federal Savings and Loan Insurance Corp. I wonder if it is too late! If they haven't changed the system yet, I may still have time to get in on a good thing.

Insurance companies have always been a mystery to me because they don't seem to work the way I always thought they were supposed to work. I was so dumb I thought that insurance was a scheme whereby many people banded together and contributed to a common kitty for the purpose of helping unfortunate members of their group restore their property after an unexpected catastrophe. If the kitty had a little extra money that wasn't needed at the moment, it was invested for the common good of the insured members of the group and also to help pay the administrative and operating expenses of managing the kitty. If the kitty ran a little short because the losses of the insured were a little greater than expected, then everybody in the group would have to contribute a little more into the kitty.

I guess the part of this whole scheme I overlooked was that it is possible to get people outside the group of the insured to pay for the losses. For instance, people who put their money into savings and loan associations are insured 100% against catastrophes because all the savings and loan associations have been putting money into a kitty to cover such losses called the FSLIC (Federal Savings and Loan Insurance Corporation). Now due to bad management (dumb investments), greed, and thefts by so many firms there isn't enough money to pay the losses of the insured. Under the current scheme of things, the government has decided that it is up to the taxpayers to sweeten the kitty to pay the losses created by the reckless gamblers and not just the insured. The government is now even talking about letting the banks in on paying the losses of the savings and loan companies by combining the FSLIC with the FDIC, which is the insurance company protecting the banks.

When I say dumb investments, this is strictly the opinion of a very ignorant observer who just can't understand why we made so many unsecured loans to third world nations who can't or won't pay them back and on whom we cannot foreclose. We do, however, foreclose on our own farmers here at home because these are secured loans and are readily accessible. It wasn't very smart to have loaned huge sums of money to underdeveloped nations in the first place, but it is ludicrous to continue to "give" more money to them after they have announced that they cannot and will not pay back either the principal or the interest.

Maybe it is just that I don't understand. Maybe we have stopped sending more money to them. Maybe some scheme has been worked out whereby the insured savings and loan companies will pay for their own losses. Maybe all these underdeveloped nations are paying back the debts with interest. Maybe the management of the savings and loan association has been changed and the new management won't make the same mistakes. Maybe the taxpayers who are not involved in this whole mess won't have to replenish the kitty. I have never before wished to be completely wrong in my thinking, and I sure hope I don't understand the situation very well this time.

I have never heard of one nation foreclosing on another nation, but they might have something we need like oil, lumber, beef, etc. that they could pay us with instead of money. One possible solution would be for the debtor nations to nationalize our holdings in their country and then sell them back to us. There's nothing new in this idea, for it's been done before. There are some nations who are rapidly destroying the world's ecological system by cutting down their rain forests. If we could swap a debt or two for a rain forest, I don't know what we'd do with the rain forest except keep it in its original state. It wouldn't help the savings and loan institutions, but they could at least go broke with a smile knowing they have done some good for the world.

If this logic is completely wrong (and I sure hope it is), just call me ignorant or sadly misinformed, but don't look for an argument from me because I'm ill equipped to defend this logic.

Just straighten out my thinking with the facts.

However, if my concept of insurance is correct, then the members of the FSLIC should raise their rates to sweeten their depleted kitty and bail out themselves.

If the management of the savings and loans were encouraged, coerced, or in someway influenced by our government to invest in these foreign countries, then it's time to get rid of the savings and loan management for being so stupid as to listen to our government on financial matters. Everybody knows our federal government has repeatedly proven it is financially incompetent. Wasn't it the federal government that set the insurance rates for the FSLIC that proved to be so inadequate?

SOLUTION: The federal government should loan funds to the FSLIC with interest to prevent its financial collapse with a finite repayment schedule. The free ride is over. It is sheer folly to ask the uninsured to pay for the losses of the insured, but who ever accused our federal government of good financial sense?

Chapter 14

SUBSIDIES

To be sure we know what we are talking about, let's see how Mr. Webster defines "subsidy." There are several definitions and, naturally, the one involving the government is the most complicated.

> Subsidy: a grant of funds or property from a government (as of the state or a municipal corporation) to a private person or company to assist in the establishment or support of an enterprise deemed advantageous to the public either as a simple gift or a payment of an amount in excess of the usual charges for a service (as in carrying the mails) or funds to aid in the establishment or maintaining a service or equipment larger or more powerful than the state of trade would warrant (as in the building and keeping in service of ships designed to use as cruisers and auxiliaries in war): broadly: an

entire payment from a government for services (as for carrying mail) which includes both compensation for actual services and a subsidy proper.

Although Mr. Webster and I agree in principal on the definition of subsidy, I describe it in different words.

Deming's definition:

Subsidy: The interruption, by the government, of the normal flow of money from consumers to sellers (producers) by taking money from consumers in the form of taxes and giving some of it to others of the government's choice (which doesn't agree with the public's desires) and keeping a substantial portion of the money for bureaucratic expenses.

It is obvious that the government is not placing the public's money where the public wants it to go because if this were the case there would be no need for the government to interrupt the normal flow of business from the buyer to the seller unless the objective is to employ more administrative bureaucrats.

Take the case of tobacco. Webster says the subsidy is money given "to a private person or company to assist in the establishment or support of an enterprise *deemed advantageous to the public.*" This is definitely untrue because, although the government subsidizes tobacco, it then spends millions of tax dollars telling consumers NOT to use it. This may make sense to the government but not to me. This action is comparable to the confused driver who doesn't know whether to go or stop, so he drives his automobile with one foot on the gas and the other foot on the brake. After spending millions of tax payers' dollars to persuade us NOT to use tobacco, the number of tobacco users in the United States has declined dramatically yet tobacco sales

14

are up. The tobacco industry has cultivated and found a very good market in foreign countries. Now I'm confused again. Could it be that the tax payers of the United States are subsidizing smokers in foreign countries? Subsidizing tobacco farmers is stupid enough but to subsidize foreign smokers is approaching the ridiculous.

I read the other day that when Nabisco acquired R. J. Reynolds, it decided to divest itself of some of the less profitable divisions of the company like food stuffs but to retain its more profitable divisions like tobacco, and yet we subsidize tobacco. Enough said?

Wheat is an entirely different situation. It is a very healthy food consumed by almost everybody in the world. I understand wheat can even be used to make a very good fuel additive which the world (except for the OPEC nations) desperately needs. So therefore we subsidize wheat farmers to grow wheat in excess of our needs so the government can buy the excess wheat and store it until Russia needs it. Then our government in it's infinite wisdom sells it to Russia at a price less than they paid to buy it, to say nothing about the storage costs. At the same time Ethiopians are starving by the hundreds of thousands. Again I'm a little puzzled as to what the objectives are in this subsidy program. Are we subsidizing the wheat farmers or Russia? There must be some logic here somewhere that has escaped me, for I am very confused (or at least somebody is confused).

The greatest subsidies of all have already been discussed in Chapter I, Income Taxes. But since the total amounts for each deduction are either unknown or unpublished, it's hard to nail them down. I think somebody doesn't want us to know.

Wholesale honey prices average about $.50 per pound

supported by about $.20 per pound subsidy. This amounts to about 40% of the cost of making honey. According to studies, the U.S. farm economy benefits $9.7 billion from honeybees. The honey output in 1988 was $107,000,000, which I calculate to be about $42,800,000 in subsidies. This amounts to $.43 of subsidy to bee keepers per $1,000.00 of farm benefits. This subsidy is such a trivial amount of money, it appears that the farmers' costs wouldn't be greatly increased if they raised their own bees. What would happen if honey wasn't subsidized? Would the bees get mad at us and fly away? Would the bees die? Would some bureaucrats be out of a job? Or would the cost of food go up .043% which is 43 cents per $1,000? If the honey subsidy were discontinued it wouldn't be all bad. Our taxes would be reduced by $42,800,000 plus the associated bureaucratic administrative expenses.

Another great subsidy that confuses me is foreign aid. The generosity of our government is so great than we have become a debtor nation. Among other things we have relieved both Germany and Japan (and many other nations) of the financial burden of supporting their own defense systems. Furthermore, in order to maintain bases to protect some of these nations such as the Philippines, we pay them for the privilege of protecting them. It would seem more logical for Germany, Japan, the Philippines, etc. to pay us for this support. We don't have to become isolationists, but it would be nice to have some friends who would support us for a change and pay their fair share of their national defense expenses. We even subsidize nations who grow narcotics and turn their heads on all efforts to stop illegal narcotic smuggling because it would hurt their economy. The whole subject of foreign aid makes me so ill, I could become at least a 90% isolationist with very little effort.

Subsidies are not all bad and unnecessary. There are even several items that we are not subsidizing that we should be subsidizing in a very big way. Let me name three — medical research (AIDS, etc.), a substitute for hydrocarbon fuels and our whole educational system. In order to increase spending in these areas we must first decide which subsidies will be reduced or eliminated. This approach to federal spending should be adopted for any expenditures over the national budget. Find the money before you spend it.

The need for additional AIDS research is so obvious that it needs no elaboration. It's merely a matter of whether we want to live or die and I've already chosen my option.

Additional funds for education is equally obvious. In many cases it is the lack of education that got us into the messes we are now discussing. These two subjects are almost without opposition. The only real resistance to spending more on these two is the fact that we don't have the money because we have already committed it to other less worthy causes.

The third subsidy I mentioned is a whole new ball game. Subsidizing research for a substitute for hydrocarbon fuels would figuratively destroy the economy of some OPEC nations, many billionaires within the United States, and some of our largest corporations. The opposition to a well-financed research program in this field would be met with such loud and well-financed opposition that it might even cause the price of oil to drop dramatically to postpone the need for such a research program. Our consumption rate of hydrocarbon fuels exceeds the earth's production rate so drastically that it is only a matter of time before the earth's hydrocarbon fuel supply is totally depleted. Whether it's fifty years or 100 years makes little difference because precious time is being wasted. Furthermore, I don't like the idea of our national defense depending on supplies from any foreigners, and Arabs in particular.

If I were in charge of a major oil company, I'd give very serious consideration to a research program for a new replaceable fuel that would eventually replace hydrocarbon fuels. Atomic energy has great promise, but it won't propel automobiles, airplanes or small boats in it's current state of development.

On February 23, 1989 a new dawn broke thanks to the generosity and good marketing strategy of Hewlett Packard. The city of Santa Monica was given a new computer which is accessible to the citizens of Santa Monica with their home computers. This idea should sweep the nation and then the federal government. When that day comes, it will be hard for the government to keep any financial secrets from the public. If everybody could get a complete printout of all subsidies and foreign aid, things might change and possibly some money could be saved. If this information is currently available, it certainly doesn't get much publicity. Like most of us, I have to have something shoved in my face with emphasis before it excites me, and it's pretty easy to hide things from me.

The solution to this subsidy problem isn't as obvious as some other problems but maybe a lot of light would help keep it under control. Many letters to our politicians asking questions which might be embarrassing would help. On the TV program "Ethics in America," the senator from Wyoming made a statement that should be repeated often concerning the swapping of votes in Congress. When congressmen get down to swapping votes in Congress, then we end up with two bad laws. This also applies to subsidies. I don't like your favorite charity, but I'll vote for it if you'll vote for mine. He said it's a rotten way to do business but it's done daily in congress and can't be stopped. It's called politics. In my book this is bribery, as well as unethical, and should be grounds for expulsion from public service, if it could be proven. With this kind of politics one could probably get a subsidy approved for white polo pony breeding, if there isn't one already. A secret ballot might stop some of the swapping so nobody would know if the other party was fulfilling his unethical bargain, but secret ballots could also hide many other things we wouldn't want hidden. Maybe a sting operation is in order.

Another possible solution is to require a separate vote for each subsidy, not a single vote for several subsidies simultaneously. No riders would be permitted on any bill.

Chapter 15

JUNK
Mail, Phone Calls, Handbills & FAX

I have lumped these four subjects together because they all come under the general classification of "invasions of privacy" which has gotten out of control. Control is not a good term because that is what is lacking. The problem is — how do we get some control of them?

JUNK MAIL

We all accept the fact that it requires a lot of money to pay the expenses of operating the U. S. Post Office, and I don't particularly object to paying my fair share of the expenses. The part I don't understand is why I have to pay $.25 per ounce for all the important mail I send out while some people are paying far less than their fair share to send me mail I object to receiving. If somebody isn't paying his fair share of the expenses, that means others are paying more than their share of the expenses. This amounts to a subsidy. Doesn't it drive you wild to think that you are subsidizing the junk mail you wish you weren't getting?

A portion of the junk mail I get is my fault for having unwittingly encouraged it and now I don't know how to turn it off. A donation to some worthy cause is a guarantee that you will receive endless cries begging for more donations in the future. They all tell you how bad the situation is now and how much worse it will be in the future if you don't help finance "The Committee To Do So and So ." After playing "soft touch" several times, I got to wondering how this money was being spent. The newspapers didn't report any significant changes in this terrible situation due to my contribution. All my inquiries for a break down of expenses and proof of some positive results have gone unanswered. Even my suggestions on how to improve their efficiency in attacking the problem and my offers to donate my services to their worthy cause have gone unanswered, which strongly indicates all they ever wanted was money. I now have formed a picture in my mind of some clerk snatching my check from the mail, putting a mark by my name on their sucker list and throwing my letter in the dumpster. I have adopted a new approach. After opening what appears to be junk mail, I scan it for the usual donation format and immediately dump it as soon as I see the option of $25 ( ), $50 ( ), etc. My junk mail has become so sophisticated that I am now receiving video tapes. I get the impression that as soon as one group finds out your sentiments on a particular subject, you are added to the mailing lists of several other groups on similar subjects and these mailing lists are sold and traded with other professional beggars.

Several years ago my U. S. Mail girl told me that any mail I receive that has the phrase "ADDRESS CORRECTION REQUESTED" on the envelope can be refused and will be sent back to the sender with first class postage due, regardless of the class of postage it was mail originally. It gave a warm feeling to think the culprits were required to pay at least twice the postage to get their junk mail back as they paid to send it to me in the first place. The idea appealed to me so much I had two rubber stamps made. The first one said ADDRESS CORREC-TION REQUESTED and the second said REFUSED. The senders of some of the junk mail I received forgot to stamp it ADDRESS CORRECTION REQUESTED, which I'm sure was an oversight on their part, so I stamped it for them and returned it. After stamping all my junk mail appropriately and returning it, I never found out what happened on the other end but my junk mail didn't seem to decrease. It just came from different sources. I think my name and address got traded like a baseball card.

Last year some bureaucrat in the California Division of Motor Vehicles decided he could raise some revenue by selling mailing lists of car owner registrations for a couple of million dollars to fatten his operating budget. Saving taxpayers some money seemed like a worthy cause, but the spontaneous negative response from the public was so loud and instantaneous the idea was abandoned the very next day after his initial press release.

The solution to this problem is not easy. The Post Office Department said it would cut off all of my mail if I had an unlisted address like an unlisted phone number. So where do we go from here? First let's discontinue bulk mailing rates so everybody pays first class rates. This won't stop all the junk mail, but at least it would give us some relief knowing we aren't subsidizing something we don't want to receive. Furthermore, it might keep the first class mail rate from increasing so rapidly.

My consultant mail girl, Sheri, said the post office department and the postal clerks' union would never support any scheme to reduce junk mail because without it half the post office employees would be out of work. Guess I don't understand the situation. I always thought the postal system was being run for the benefit of the public rather than the postal workers. Wrong again!

Another part of the solution would be to require that all junk mail could be refused and returned to sender at the sender's expense (first class rates postage due). A third possible solution would be to indicate in some manner, such as putting a "P" before our address, indicating this is a personal address and make it unlawful to put any such address on mailing lists. Of course, if your name happens to be P. Resident you are still in trouble.

These solutions are nothing to be proud of, but this is a desperate situation and no other practical solution comes to mind.

JUNK PHONE CALLS

"You have been computer selected from a very exclusive list of people in your area to receive our special offer."

"Hello Mr. Jones, how are you today? I'm calling from the Hometown Gazette with a very special offer for new subscribers." (I already take their paper).

Do these phrases sound familiar? These telephone solicitors have a sixth sense to know when you are eating dinner, in the shower or other times when answering the phone is most inconvenient or undesirable. This situation is not as bad as junk mail yet, but with solicitors now calling long distance from New

York and Florida to California you know it's getting worse. People with unlisted phone numbers aren't safe any more and are now getting these calls also.

Have you ever wondered who was calling you to conduct surveys and "telemarketing"? The following is a news clipping from the *Sacramento Union* dated July 8, 1990 (from the *Minneapolis-St. Paul Star Tribune*).

> At Shakopee prison, 10 female inmates paid by the state do telephone market surveys of Twin Cities-based Super Valu Stores. Among the questions put to shoppers nationwide: Where do you shop? Do you use coupons? What stores offer the best quality of meat? Best selection of produce?
>
> The telemarketing program expanded last month when it began a fund-raising campaign for a camp in Brainerd, Minn., for handicapped people.
>
> Shakopee inmates are paid 55 cents per hour during an initial month-long training period, then an hourly wage of up to $2.25, based on the number of completed surveys. A portion of their wages are withheld for taxes and a victim's assistance fund. And, like most other workers, inmates can accrue vacation and sick time, and they can get fired.

Giving prisoners some on-the-job training is a very good idea, however teaching them the art and skill of invading privacy is questionable and a waste of time. Some of them are already too experienced in the art of invasion of privacy which is what got them into prison. Shakopee prison is not an isolated case. The news article continues:

Prisoners at the Arizona women's prison in Phoenix have done a good portion of hotel reservations for Best Western since 1981. Arizona inmates also take telephone ticket sales for NBA basketball games, Ice Capades shows, rock concerts, and other events for the Dillard department store chain in Arizona, Colorado, Nevada and New Mexico. Officials said the prison is now looking for contracts with car-rental companies.

Fighting unwanted sales and survey calls is very difficult because the callers will rarely disclose their telephone number. However, now that Shakopee prison has been identified, some people may want to retaliate with some nuisance calls of their own to the warden at very inconvenient hours.

There is a significant difference between the two prison programs. Shakopee prison is promoting the invasion of our privacy whereas Arizona women's prison is performing a service. Wake up, Shakopee prison, you are promoting what I call a crime.

Hope fighting a prison isn't as tough as fighting city hall!

The solution here is much easier than for junk mail. Just raise your voice a little and say, "Get off the phone! I'm trying to call an ambulance." This is a very temporary fix, because you will remain on their list for future calls. A little more effective approach is to sound interested and ask them to tell you all about their promotion, then quietly lay the phone down without hanging up and abandon it until you hear the phone company's "off the hook" signal. This beats hanging up in their face, because this procedure wastes their time and destroys their calling efficiency, whereas hanging up saves them time. For those who are selling precious metals, bonds, etc. you tell them "whoever put my name on your call list was pulling your leg because I'm living strictly on Social Security and not making it, good bye!"

For the really persistent callers (e.g. literally dozens of phone calls soliciting subscriptions for our local newspaper), I am inventing a new product to be called "Blab Off." It is simply a little plastic box that sits on the table next to the phone which fits the mouth piece and the earpiece and produces a loud shrill shriek called "feedback" when the phone is placed on the box. Childish, but I'm confident it will get us off their lists.

HANDBILLS

In the Elementary Burglary and House Break-in Course 1A, they teach the first thing to do when planning a break-in is to cruise the targeted neighborhood looking for telltale signs of occupants not at home. Handbills in the front driveway or porch are the number one thing to look for. Newspapers can be stopped or picked up by the neighbors, but handbills can't be stopped. These handbills are more than just an annoyance, they are dangerous to the safety of our homes. If the burglar's basic requirement of handbills has been met, look for other telltale signs like no lights at night, lights left on in the daytime, curtains drawn in the daytime, overgrown lawns, sprinklers running in the rain, etc., but remember always to look for the handbills first.

Things we don't have any use for are called trash and are discarded. There should be some way to discourage others from throwing trash in our yards. Maybe if we reserved a special trash container for all those handbill goodies and saved them for the proper occasion, they might be turned into profit. The proper occasion would be when the house is robbed and a class action suit is filed against everybody whose handbills are in the goodie barrel. Even in small claims court at about $1500.00 a throw, it could mount up to a pretty tidy sum. Anybody want to give it a try and let me know the results?

There are signs along our highways cautioning a "$500 FINE FOR LITTERING." If littering public lands carries such a steep fine, why shouldn't littering private property be protected equally well? My new business in retirement might be to sell anti littering signs for private residences along with my "BLAB OFF."

JUNK FAX MESSAGES

I hear junk FAX messages are the latest thing and rapidly becoming a nuisance. My solution to this is — don't own a FAX machine. Some day when I catch up with this sophisticated world and get to know the problem first hand, I'll give it some thought.

Chapter 16

ELECTIONS

Who's steering the ship of state? There are several schools of thought on this subject. When Barry Goldwater was running for president in about 1963 he was quizzed on a TV program called *Face The Nation* as to who really runs the nation? His reply was that it's not the president, nor congress, nor big business, nor big labor, nor the bankers, it's the bureaucrats in Washington, D.C. We elect their leaders but they run the nation. As stated before, when Jerry Brown first took office as governor of California, he said his first big shock was when he discovered he only had the power to fire six state employees — his chauffeur and some of his office staff.

So if the bureaucrats really run this nation, who is it that selects our politicians? Some say it is the people, but let's analyze this to see who really selects the political leaders. We all seem to fall into at least one of the many voter groups listed on the following page.

Die hard Democrats
"My family has always voted democratic and always will."

Die hard Republicans
"There's only one way to vote and that's mine."

The "who cares" party
"Why even register? My vote won't count — I'd rather complain."

Splinter groups:

Emotionalists — one issue voters (e.g. abortion, death penalty)
"I don't know how he stands on other issues as long as he supports or fights my big issue."

Winners
"Be with the winner — Jack will win so I'll vote for him."

Apathetics
"I don't have time to vote — nothing will change anyway."

Hawks & Doves
"The paranoids & the flower children (pacifists)."

Antagonists
"Our president and congress should be of different parties — let's watch them fight."

Big vs. Little Gov't
"Leave me alone" vs. "They must do more for me."

Incumbents
"At least we know what were getting."

Peace and Freedom, Libertarians, American Nazi Party,

Communists, etc. and the list goes on. Most splinter group members talk their party platform but realize their vote is wasted if they ultimately don't vote democratic or republican. In their case, "close counts" when voting for the candidate who comes closest to their splinter group platform gets the vote.

Some say it is the people who select our politicians. Wrong. It is only some of the people, and it's a very small minority who actually control the average election. Let's analyze the outcome of a typical election. In the following illustration, all numbers are assumptions, so don't be mislead by their inaccuracy.

Total population of the country 250,000,000

Registered voters 125,000,000

Actual voters (about 40%) 50,000,000

Splinter groups (about 5%) 2,500,000

That leaves voting Republicans & Democrats. 47,500,000

Take away the die-hard solid voters whose families have voted the straight ticket for several generations. Their vote is very predictable and tends to offset the other. The only uncertainty is whether or not they will vote:

Democrats 23,000,000

Republicans 19,500,000

That leaves the objective voters who study
the candidates and issues before voting 5,000,000

These 5,000,000 voters are only about 2% of the population of this country. They include the single issue voters, who vote for only the highly publicized and emotional issues and candidates, not everything on the ballot, and if nothing stirs their emotions they don't bother to vote. In spite of our dissatisfaction with the spending habits of our public officials, the incumbents are consistently returned to our over-spending government in the overwhelming majority of cases.

Does it worry you that about 2% of our population actually runs this nation the majority of the time? Maybe your vote is more important than you think it is. Where do you fit in now? Just think, if you aren't an active voter at present, you could get off your complacency and become one of the 2% who runs this nation.

Who should vote? About 350 BC, Plato discussed the rulers of his ideal state and their development. He classified people in three groups depending on their age and desires.

a)   reason   rulers

b)   emotional or spirited   military

c)   desire   craftsmen

Ages and their training:

0 - 18   training in literature, music and some mathematics

18 - 20   intensive military training

20 - 30   some advanced courses in mathematics

30 - 35   dialectic

35 - 50   practical experience for ruling

50 - up   philosopher-rulers, ruling and guiding the state

The only point in bringing up Plato is that he recognized that those who made decisions effecting the state needed a lot of experience and training before they become rulers and are allowed to vote.

To a small child "hot" is a word, and no matter how hard

you try to explain "hot" it is still just a word until the child touches a hot stove, then the word "hot" takes on a true meaning to the child due to experience. We all know the old cliché "there's no substitute for experience," and yet we totally ignored our own good judgment in 1969 when we lowered the voting age to eighteen years of age. I wrote a letter to my senator at that time, George Murphy, urging him to vote against the measure to lower the voting age, and pointed out about 50 simple, very ordinary and common experiences that 99% of all eighteen year olds have not had, such as the following:

paid income taxes	been audited by the IRS
had to find a job	had to buy all their clothes
had to support themselves	been fired from a job
been legally intoxicated	been married
been divorced	had children
bought a car	owned a credit card
hired a lawyer	supported dependent parents
buried a close relative	had military experience
survived a depression	filed an insurance claim
paid rent	bought a house

It would be easier to list the experiences the average eighteen-year-old has had, rather than try to complete the list of experiences they have not had.

I sent a copy of my three page letter to all ninety six senators and received seventeen replies. Three of the replies (one from Senator George McGovern) were incorrect form letters thanking me for supporting their bill to lower the voting age to eighteen years of age. It is disheartening to think our political leaders base their opinions on these inaccurate tallies of the letters they receive from us. Could it be that their staff is deliberately misleading them? Three wrong out of seventeen adds up to an 18% error which could sway almost any election. I wrote George McGovern a scathing letter of dissatisfaction, accusing him of being incapable of reading, and suggested he was unqualified for his job along with some other obnoxious suggestions. I received another reply (this time from George instead of an incorrect form letter) suggesting that my immoderate language was not the way to put my point across. Chalk up two points for George. He was right about my language and, secondly, he got his bill through Congress and the totally inexperienced kids can now vote. I'm sure he expected to capture the naïve "kid" vote. (But I got the satisfaction of getting his full attention with my second letter instead of another wrong form letter.)

I personally think the voting age should be raised to about forty or fifty so voters would have had many good and bad experiences and hopefully learned in the process. Unfortunately, that bridge has been completely burned, and it will never be rebuilt during my lifetime. It is inconceivable that any politician could or would convince a majority to vote for a proposition that would take away their vote.

In every election we have many campaigns to "get out and vote." These campaigns appear to be all-inclusive but they are almost always directed at a particular block of voters. The Republicans want other Republicans to get out and vote, the Democrats want their group to vote, the blacks, the browns, the pinks, the young, the old, all want their group to vote. Someday maybe we'll have a better slogan like "Study the Ballot

THEN Get Out and Vote." Voting for an incumbent is quite often the result of voters voting for a known versus an unknown candidate even if we don't know his past voting record and haven't taken the time to study the alternatives.

There is no simple solution to these voting problems. Maybe if the rules were changed to preclude any political officeholder from being elected to an office more than two terms, we'd have to be more alert when selecting his replacement and stop returning some of the big spenders to our nation's spending department (Congress). Maybe if we limited retired politicians to one pension it would slow down a few. When last I heard, Senator Alan Cranston of California was still serving in the Senate and simultaneously drawing six government pensions plus allowances. There should be a limit to the number of governmental pensions one can draw and pension payments should start at a retirement age, not immediately.

There are two other problems in our voting procedure that we should correct immediately and very simply. First of all, if all primary elections were held the same day, the vote from one state couldn't effect the outcome of the vote in other states. Momentum would no longer be a factor and there wouldn't be any pivotal states. The single primary election should be about three weeks before the general election. Hopefully this would cut down on the cost and time spent campaigning and allow more time for constructive work.

The second problem is the staggered voting times between the east coast and Hawaii due to time zones. Currently the national election has been decided while the Hawaiians are still voting. Let's vote 100% by mail as absentee voting is done now. This would eliminate the time differential and would save money. The postage cost of mailing ballots is probably much less than the cost of transportation getting millions of voters to the polls. Today, you can't back your car out of the garage for the price of a postage stamp.

Several times in our history we have had a president and congress from different political parties and consequently nothing is accomplished but political in fighting. A typical example was when Herbert Hoover, a Republican president, tried unsuccessfully to get his PWA program funded by a Democratic congress. So the great depression continued. His successor Franklin Roosevelt, a Democratic president, renamed the program WPA, which was heavily funded by his Democratic congress. Perhaps we should give some serious study to the British system where the political head of state is elected by the governing body. This would assure the cooperation of these two bodies to some degree.

Check your own reasoning the next time you vote to see in which category of voter you are. Does your vote really count or are you in one of the automatic and predictable classes that tend to offset each other? Are you driving with one foot on the gas and the other on the brake by voting for different parties for congress and the presidency? If you aren't, somebody is, because we have a republican president and democratic congress.

An alternative would be to have three major political parties. Then we could have one dominate the senate, one dominate the house of representatives and the third one for the presidency. This would assure us that absolutely nothing constructive or destructive would ever be accomplished. Make sense?

Before leaving this very important subject, I have three

possible election changes that are worthy of your consideration.

Let's close all the polls and take the simplest one first. The manner in which we *do not* vote in the United States is truly a disgrace. People all over the world are risking their lives daily for the privilege of voting, and we in the United States usually get about a 40% turnout of those who even bother to register to vote. We cannot force people to vote, but we can offer them several incentives to go to the polls and hope they will make an effort to prepare themselves for a sincere vote. Remember the last time you voted they tore off a little stub from your ballot and handed it to you as evidence that you had voted. If this stub were worth about a $25 or $50 tax deduction on the dreaded April 15th income tax day, I believe our voting turnout would improve substantially. Like most good ideas, there is a little flaw to this one which I think will prove to be too minor to detract from its success. All the skid row junkies might register and vote just to get the ballot stub which they could trade for a bottle of cheap wine or a drink at their favorite watering hole. Even with this possibility, I think the idea has merit and the penalties for income tax fraud are severe enough to eliminate this crime.

The next suggested election change is to have all ballots printed with one more voting option for political offices entitled "NONE OF THE ABOVE." If "NONE OF THE ABOVE" won an election or prevented one candidate from getting a majority vote, there would have to be a court-appointed caretaker to run the office pending another election. Voting for "NONE OF THE ABOVE" would be much more meaningful than not showing up at the polls. This also provides an opportunity to vote "NO" on those candidates who run unopposed on the ballot and consequently do not expose their views or records by campaigning.

The third change for you to ponder is to let the voters have some control over the salary of the winning politician. If a politician wins an election by a huge majority, he certainly represents a larger portion of the voting public than a politician who won his office by a fraction of a percentage point and should be paid more. Let's build a hypothetical case. Note, this whole idea is confined to those political offices where there is competition, eliminating unopposed candidates and judgeships. I have set the current base salary of our hypothetical political office at $100,000 per year. The winning candidate's salary would be increased by a bonus salary depending upon his margin of victory. The purpose of this sliding scale bonus salary is to encourage voters to vote for their candidate even when they are extremely confident he will win and to vote against candidates they do not want elected instead of taking the attitude that "my vote won't count" because the undesirable candidate is favored by a large majority. A vote for the underdog may not defeat the undesirable candidate, but at least the winning candidate will know there are many who do not support him and his salary scale will reflect their displeasure. Every vote counts even in defeat. Even "NONE OF THE ABOVE" would play an important part of every election and contribute to adjusting the salary of the winning candidate. Every vote is either a plus or minus to the politician's salary.

The following chart is an illustration of how this might happen:

Winning Margin	Bonus Salary (%)	Bonus Salary ($)	Base Salary	Total Salary
1%	2%	$2,000	$100,000	$102,000
2%	4%	$4,000	$100,000	$104,000
3%	6%	$6,000	$100,000	$106,000
4%	8%	$8,000	$100,000	$108,000
5%	10%	$10,000	$100,000	$110,000
6%	13%	$13,000	$100,000	$113,000
7%	16%	$16,000	$100,000	$116,000
8%	19%	$19,000	$100,000	$119,000
9%	22%	$22,000	$100,000	$122,000
10%	25%	$25,000	$100,000	$125,000
12%	29%	$29,000	$100,000	$129,000
14%	33%	$33,000	$100,000	$133,000
16%	37%	$37,000	$100,000	$137,000
18%	41%	$41,000	$100,000	$141,000
20% & Up	50%	$50,000	$100,000	$150,000

Winning an election is only part of the game — by how much is also important and this is where every vote counts. The election results would reflect the true sentiments of the voters. This also would drive the TV and newspaper political pollsters nuts.

Chapter 17

ILLEGAL ALIENS

I guess I was wallowing in complacency or partially asleep when "illegal" became "acceptable" and ultimately Congress decided to change "illegal" to "legal" when they set up their amnesty program for *illegal aliens*. Just when we thought it couldn't get any worse, it did. The old adage "if you can't beat them, join them" has become a way of life with Congress. There is no right or wrong, it's all compromise. In it's infinite wisdom, Congress decided that those aliens who have sneaked into this country illegally, taken up residence, found employment (or welfare), and have successfully evaded the law for a given length of time shall have their crime rewarded by being reclassified as "legal" if they register with the INS (Immigration & Naturalization Service). They were given 18 months to take advantage of this offer. The illegal aliens didn't exactly jump at this amnesty gesture, so David Ilchert, San Francisco Director of the INS, announced "anyone who's a temporary resident, start applying now, don't worry about the 18 months." He sounds like he is working on a commission and getting paid by the alien.

The following is a March 2, 1989 clipping from the United Press International:

"Under Phase I of the amnesty program, 1.765 million illegal aliens qualified for temporary residency between May 5, 1987 and May 4, 1988. Phase II, in which the aliens could apply for permanent residence began last November.

To qualify for permanent residency status, applicants must have completed 40 hours of a 60 hour INS-approved course of study in basic English and American history and government or pass the INS video proficiency test."

It is interesting to note that May 5 (Cinco de Mayo) is to Mexico what the 4th of July is to the United States.

Some illegal aliens feared it was a trap to get them to expose themselves. Some didn't even hear of the amnesty program. Others felt "why bother, the INS is helpless and doesn't offer much threat to us, so why register?" But worse yet, they have demonstrated they don't want to learn basic English or anything about our history or government and don't give a hoot about our laws.

The amnesty program should have at least included a Phase III probationary period of one year requiring a perfect citizenship record.

It won't be long until the illegal aliens and their "legal" offsprings who automatically become citizens will outnumber the citizenry in Florida, Texas, Arizona, New Mexico and California (if they haven't already), so this might be the most peaceful way of solving this ugly situation we have allowed to develop.

Where will all this lead us? Will Congress decide to solve our over crowded prison situation the same way by giving amnesty to all convicts, open the prison doors and welcome the convicts back into our society so the pardoned prisoners can get a fresh start at overloading the prisons again? With this kind of thinking, we won't have to fear overcrowded prisons again because this philosophy might even get to a point where we will have a national holiday called "Amnesty Day." Hope this doesn't give any ideas to those bleeding hearts who blame society and the innocent victims of crime rather than the lawbreakers for the actions of the guilty criminals and want to do away with death row. It all fits part of the politicians creed that a little crime is okay and should be overlooked.

The lesson to be learned here is — don't let things get out of hand. World War II could have been avoided if things weren't allowed to get out of hand. Don't misinterpret this remark because in no way am I implying that our illegal alien problem could result in a catastrophic war the magnitude of World War II, however we are losing our nation and our way of life.

This deplorable illegal alien situation came about because we have a law that is unenforceable under the current circumstances. The Immigration & Naturalization Service (INS) border guards are unfortunately outnumbered, out gunned and now outmaneuvered by our politicians. They don't stand a chance.

Most of us enjoy people born in a foreign land who have decided to accept and adopt our culture, freedom and principles upon which our nation has been operating. We were all aliens at one time except for the American Indians who didn't control their illegal alien immigration problem and let things get out of hand, and look at them now. What we do not enjoy are foreigners who invade us to set up colonies within the United States, refuse to speak our language and bring with them consciously or subconsciously the culture and problems they say they wanted to leave behind them. There are portions of some states where one gets the feeling they are entering a foreign country. The Cubans, Mexicans, Vietnamese, Japanese, etc. all gather in their own colonies and start feuding with other colonies.

An outstanding example was the invasion of a small Oregon community by the Bhagwan Shree Rajneesh and his followers. In a very short period of time they had the native Oregonians outnumbered and systematically set about changing all the laws to suit themselves. They literally captured the whole community and if it wasn't for being guilty of immigration fraud and being deported, he would still be there ruling part of Oregon.

President Theodore Roosevelt wanted to do away with "hyphenated Americans." No more Italian-Americans, German-Americans, Mexican-Americans, etc., they're all Americans and they should understand that when they decide to enter our country. President Teddy wouldn't be at all pleased with today's situation. We have dropped the hyphen and the American instead of the hyphen and the foreign part of the phrase. Instead of Mexican-American it is now Mexican or Vietnamese or Cuban, exactly the reverse of what he wanted.

The *San Francisco Chronicle* reported that the San Francisco school system is composed of 83% foreign and minority students. It also has the highest high school dropout rate of 43.1% as opposed to 22.7% for the state and the national rate of 27.0%. Has it occurred to you how much we have distorted the meaning of the word "minority"? How can the remaining 17% of the high school students in San Francisco be considered the majority or did they redefine that word too while I was napping? A southern white politician asked a black man, "What should we do about the black problem?" The black man replied, "We don't have a black problem, we have a white problem." It looks like we have lost track of what has happened while we were sleeping.

In my opinion we have lost control of the immigration situation and are rapidly losing our country. All of these illegal aliens are making babies at a prodigious rate who are automatically U. S. citizens growing up without the normal citizenship requirements of learning to speak basic English, some American history, some knowledge of the constitution, etc. They certainly won't learn it from their illegal alien parents. A few of these native born citizens will learn some of this in school but not many with the high drop out rate. We used to call our nation a melting pot where many nationalities were blended into a nation but we have let the fire burn out under the pot so the ingredients are still separated.

Getting control will be very difficult but if it is to happen, we must start some place. A good start should be the 2000 mile long Mexican border. This border is a boulevard of fast moving traffic of illegal aliens including many drug smugglers running in the pack.

In the January 25, 1989 *San Francisco Chronicle* the INS announced plans to build an earth and concrete ditch 14 feet wide and 5 feet deep running along the border for about five miles east of the main border crossing at San Ysidro, California. Government officials estimate that 300 to 400 vehicles cross the border illegally in the San Diego border area every month. The isolated terrain that separates Tijuana, Mexico from San

Diego, California accounted for more than one third of the 1,200,000 illegal immigrants apprehended along the U.S.-Mexico border last year. The ditch plan offended Mexico. Arnoldo Torres, national political director for the League of United Latin American Citizens, called the plan "shocking, for it takes on desperate proportions and will have negative consequences, symbolically as well as suspensively" — whatever that means. To me this takes on the flavor of bank robbers being offended by banks locking their doors and vaults.

But a Bush administration official, noting the distinctions between the fence and the ditch said, "This is going to work to the extent that it will keep vehicles out. This is not intended to stop people from crossing on foot. Unlike the fence, this is not something that can be easily damaged or destroyed." Apparently he doesn't understand the problem and thinks it's illegal vehicles that threatens our way of life.

The ditch sounds like a good idea to me, but it will take many more additional good ideas to correct this deplorable situation. Walls, ditches, fences and beefing up the INS is all that I can suggest, but the amnesty program definitely is not the answer. Allowing thieves to keep their booty if they can evade the law for a prescribed length of time sounds to me more like an incentive to crime rather than a deterrent and the amnesty program is just as ridiculous. The amnesty program falls into that lunacy category of repealing all laws so we won't have any law-breakers. At least this idea would solve our lawyer overabundance problem. No laws = no lawyers. When the penalty for breaking into our country is a free ride home, it certainly hasn't been much of a deterrent.

Chapter 18

THE LOTTERY LIE

Several states in the United States have legalized state sanctioned gambling in their respective states under the guise of supporting some very worthy causes. Gambling has a very bad name because of it's known or suspected association with a pretty rowdy element of our society that is suspected of violent crimes and illegal acts to control their very lucrative enterprises. Of course, we don't have to worry about these dangers as long as we have state politicians running this legalized gambling, because we know they're honest and won't tolerate any hanky-panky.

In California we have the 6/49 LOTTO which is the legalized form of gambling whereby the player tries to pick six correct numbers out of a field of forty-nine numbers. If successful he will win the Lotto jackpot, which is about five million dollars every Wednesday and Saturday for starters. The winning jackpot is paid over a period of twenty years in equal payments. Of course, if more than one person picks the six correct numbers all winning players share the jackpot equally. If nobody picks the six correct numbers, the money (jackpot or purse) is then added to the next jackpot which will be either the following Wednesday or Saturday. Again, if there is no winner the money is added to the next jackpot. On several occasions the jackpot has exceeded $50,000,000.00 before somebody or a group of somebodies has picked the correct six numbers.

Some Lotto players feel their chances of winning a huge jackpot is diminished because they must compete with so many other gamblers. The odds of winning when the jackpot has grown to a huge number are identical to the odds of winning a smaller jackpot. The only change in the situation is that there will probably be several winners to share the big prize. It has been my observation that those who share a huge jackpot end up with about the same amount of money as a single winner of a smaller jackpot.

The downside of this justified gambling scheme is that the sole justification for all this gambling is to enhance the state's school budget. Either our school officials are a greedy bunch of ingrates grumbling about the money they receive or a significant portion of the money intended for the schools isn't finding its intended purpose.

We're talking about some really big money. Like the late Senator Dirksen once said to his newly elected senator son-in-law (Senator Howard Baker), "a million here and a million there and pretty soon we're talking about some real money" (being a federal senator, he used the term BILLION). For sake of illustration, let us assume you have won a jackpot of $10,000,000.00. If you were the sole winner you would be paid your jackpot in equal annual payments of $500,000 each over the next twenty years.

A $10,000,000.00 jackpot sounds fantastic, but what is it really worth? Let us assume the state really has the money to pay it all to you now (and I have no idea whether they do or do not). They aren't going to let go of it all at once. Under the current rules, they appear to have at least three alternatives.

Their first alternative is to invest "your" money in an annuity at 8% which pays twenty $500,000 payments and ends up with a zero balance after twenty years. That's assuming they really have the money. How much does this annuity cost them? According to the following chart it is only worth $4,909,073.71 today (see figure 1), which is the real value of your alleged $10,000,000.00 jackpot. Less than half of what they said you had won.

The second alternative is to invest $6,250,000 in municipal tax-free bonds at 8% which pay interest at $500,000 per year. At the end of twenty years, you have been paid "your $10,000,000.00" (twenty payments of $500,000 each) from the interest on the bonds and the state still has all of their original principal investment and has lost nothing (see figure 2).

The third alternative, which is most probably the one being pursued by the state, is to invest nothing and pay the winners from current income being invested by potential future Lotto winners. If you operated a bank or business this way, your immediate and long term future would be in the slammer. Who said politicians are dumb and don't know how to handle money. This has got to be the champion flimflam of all time and is really a sucker's game.

If you had really won $10,000,000 and the state, in its superior financial wisdom, invested your money and doled it out to you over a twenty year period with its earned interest, your

FIGURE 1

LOTTO ALTERNATIVE NUMBER ONE

8% ANNUITY FOR PAYMENTS TOTALING $10,000,000.00

YEAR	PRINCIPAL	INTEREST	BALANCE	PAYMENT	BALANCE
1	$4,909,073.71	$392,726	$5,301,800	$500,000	$4,801,800
2	$4,801,799.61	$384,144	$5,185,944	$500,000	$4,685,944
3	$4,685,943.58	$374,875	$5,060,819	$500,000	$4,560,819
4	$4,560,819.06	$364,866	$4,925,685	$500,000	$4,425,685
5	$4,425,684.59	$354,055	$4,779,739	$500,000	$4,279,739
6	$4,279,739.35	$342,379	$4,622,118	$500,000	$4,122,118
7	$4,122,118.50	$329,769	$4,451,888	$500,000	$3,951,888
8	$3,951,887.98	$316,151	$4,268,039	$500,000	$3,768,039
9	$3,768,039.02	$301,443	$4,069,482	$500,000	$3,569,482
10	$3,569,482.14	$285,559	$3,855,041	$500,000	$3,355,041
11	$3,355,040.71	$268,403	$3,623,444	$500,000	$3,123,444
12	$3,123,443.97	$249,876	$3,373,319	$500,000	$2,873,319
13	$2,873,319.49	$229,866	$3,103,185	$500,000	$2,603,185
14	$2,603,185.05	$208,255	$2,811,440	$500,000	$2,311,440
15	$2,311,439.85	$184,915	$2,496,355	$500,000	$1,996,355
16	$1,996,355.04	$159,708	$2,156,063	$500,000	$1,656,063
17	$1,656,063.44	$132,485	$1,788,549	$500,000	$1,288,549
18	$1,288,548.52	$103,084	$1,391,632	$500,000	$891,632
19	$891,632.40	$71,331	$962,963	$500,000	$462,963
20	$462,962.99	$37,037	$500,000	$500,000	$0

FIGURE 2

LOTTO ALTERNATIVE NUMBER TWO

8% FUND

YEAR	PRINCIPAL	INTEREST	BALANCE	PAYMENT	BALANCE
1	$6,250,000.00	$500,000	$6,750,000	$500,000	$6,250,000
2	$6,250,000.00	$500,000	$6,750,000	$500,000	$6,250,000
3	$6,250,000.00	$500,000	$6,750,000	$500,000	$6,250,000
4	$6,250,000.00	$500,000	$6,750,000	$500,000	$6,250,000
5	$6,250,000.00	$500,000	$6,750,000	$500,000	$6,250,000
6	$6,250,000.00	$500,000	$6,750,000	$500,000	$6,250,000
7	$6,250,000.00	$500,000	$6,750,000	$500,000	$6,250,000
8	$6,250,000.00	$500,000	$6,750,000	$500,000	$6,250,000
9	$6,250,000.00	$500,000	$6,750,000	$500,000	$6,250,000
10	$6,250,000.00	$500,000	$6,750,000	$500,000	$6,250,000
11	$6,250,000.00	$500,000	$6,750,000	$500,000	$6,250,000
12	$6,250,000.00	$500,000	$6,750,000	$500,000	$6,250,000
13	$6,250,000.00	$500,000	$6,750,000	$500,000	$6,250,000
14	$6,250,000.00	$500,000	$6,750,000	$500,000	$6,250,000
15	$6,250,000.00	$500,000	$6,750,000	$500,000	$6,250,000
16	$6,250,000.00	$500,000	$6,750,000	$500,000	$6,250,000
17	$6,250,000.00	$500,000	$6,750,000	$500,000	$6,250,000
18	$6,250,000.00	$500,000	$6,750,000	$500,000	$6,250,000
19	$6,250,000.00	$500,000	$6,750,000	$500,000	$6,250,000
20	$6,250,000.00	$500,000	$6,750,000	$500,000	$6,250,000

annual payments would be $1,018,522.09, which is considerably more than the $500,000 the winner would get today (see figure 3).

I wish the state would let me pay my debts to them the same way they are paying the Lotto winners. You may not think these figures are correct, but I am absolutely positive of what I say and will pay $1,000,000.00 to the first person to prove my figures are not absolutely correct (at the rate of $1.00 per year for the next one million years, which is the state's payment philosophy).

Today is Wednesday and I'm happy to have finished this chapter so I can turn on the TV to see if I have won this week's Lotto. I'm not necessarily against all gambling, but I am *vehemently* opposed to false advertising and being lied to by our elected officials.

FIGURE 3

LOTTO ALTERNATIVE NUMBER FOUR

8% FUND – TWENTY PAYMENTS OF $1,018,522.09 = $20,370,442

YEAR	PRINCIPAL	INTEREST	BALANCE	PAYMENT	BALANCE
1	$10,000,000	$800,000	$10,800,000	$1,018,522.09	$9,781,478
2	$9,781,478	$782,518	$10,563,996	$1,018,522.09	$9,545,474
3	$9,545,474	$763,638	$10,309,112	$1,018,522.09	$9,290,590
4	$9,290,590	$743,247	$10,033,837	$1,018,522.09	$9,015,315
5	$9,015,315	$721,225	$9,736,540	$1,018,522.09	$8,718,018
6	$8,718,018	$697,441	$9,415,459	$1,018,522.09	$8,396,937
7	$8,396,937	$671,755	$9,068,692	$1,018,522.09	$8,050,170
8	$8,050,170	$644,014	$8,694,184	$1,018,522.09	$7,675,662
9	$7,675,662	$614,053	$8,289,715	$1,018,522.09	$7,271,193
10	$7,271,193	$581,695	$7,852,888	$1,018,522.09	$6,834,366
11	$6,834,366	$546,749	$7,381,115	$1,018,522.09	$6,362,593
12	$6,362,593	$509,007	$6,871,600	$1,018,522.09	$5,853,078
13	$5,853,079	$468,246	$6,321,325	$1,018,522.09	$5,302,803
14	$5,302,803	$424,224	$5,727,027	$1,018,522.09	$4,708,505
15	$4,708,505	$376,680	$5,085,185	$1,018,522.09	$4,066,663
16	$4,066,663	$325,333	$4,391,996	$1,018,522.09	$3,373,474
17	$3,373,474	$269,878	$3,643,352	$1,018,522.09	$2,624,830
18	$2,624,830	$209,986	$2,834,816	$1,018,522.09	$1,816,294
19	$1,816,294	$145,304	$1,961,598	$1,018,522.09	$943,075
20	$943,076	$75,446	$1,018,522	$1,018,522.09	$0

Chapter 19

THE TOTAL PERSONAL MANAGER

This subject is so complicated that it really deserves an entire book to cover it properly. It is my favorite idea which is really a prediction so inevitable it will happen eventually. The time and computer technology is already here to make this idea feasible, however almost all the large firms who can handle this managerial type of business would have a conflict of interest the way they are structured now. What makes it so complicated is that it is actually many subjects or problems boiled into one. My first problem is where to start to describe it.

One day while working in aerospace, I was summoned to the boss's office and told of a major problem which had occurred in our company. We had just been notified by the government that one of our programs had been terminated. When President John Kennedy announced emphatically to the world that we were going to have a man on the moon within the decade it resulted in a major CRASH PROGRAM. A crash program, as defined by one of our scientists, is like an accelerated pregnancy. If it takes one woman nine months to produce a baby, then we'll assign nine women to the job and get it done in one month. The government's philosophy, though costly, wasn't entirely wrong when it awarded competing contracts to several different firms to accomplish the same job, knowing that only the one showing the best promise, after a designated length of time, would be destined to finish the job. Such a philosophy presented a marvelous opportunity for in-house politics (within the government) and far too much money being spent, but this is the price of crash programs. We had a competing contract and our product exceeded our competitor's product in weight, reliability, performance, cost, etc. so we were very confident in its future and that we would be the lone survivor of the competition, however the other firm was selected to finish the job. I only bring up these sour grapes because it explains why we were so totally unprepared for the dreaded telegram stating "government contract number 12345 is hereby terminated."

"Termination" is a governmental contractual term which means to stop all work immediately (not someday, but right now this very instant), bundle up all drawings, reports, hardware regardless of the state of completion, inventory the whole mess, crate it and ship it to a government termination warehouse. The boss told me to turn my department over to my assistant and work full time on this terminated contract, and when the job was completed, I could have my department back. I explained that I had absolutely no experience in contract terminations and that they should give this assignment to an expert in this field. The problem was that we had never had a contract terminated before, consequently nobody had any experience. It was my hot potato.

The first thing to do was to familiarize myself with the program and immediately, that day, lay off 685 employees who were working on the program, most of whom were engineering personnel. It meant shuffling senior personnel to other projects which triggered an internal game of musical chairs that cascaded throughout the entire company with no place to hide for the junior employees. Other than turmoil, the problem didn't appear too serious on the surface because another aerospace company only five miles away was eagerly looking for good engineering personnel.

Here comes the rub. We were forced to lay off personnel, the unneeded personnel wanted to move to where the future was brighter, and the other aerospace firm needed most of the personnel. This instantaneously created an individual personnel shock. To change companies meant a loss of seniority, loss of retirement benefits, loss of health benefits, changing credit unions, reduction in managerial status, loss of seniority vacation time, loss of fringe benefits and in many cases a temporary loss of income. These things have happened many times in the past and will happen again in the future, so if they are expected, why can't we prepare for them in some way by devising a system that permits the mobility of labor without penalty? Which brings me to the grand solution. The grand solution solves many of these problems and many more not yet mentioned.

But first, let's analyze the real problem. When I was a very young boy on a tour of the California Institute of Technology campus our guide pointed out a man walking across the campus eating an ice cream cone. It was Professor Albert Einstein, who was already a famous celebrity and almost a curiosity because of some of his eccentricities. A newspaper reporter asked him many personal questions and got some unexpected answers. It turned out that he didn't know to the nearest decimal point what his salary was and didn't give it much thought because his wife was his manager who paid all the bills, and he felt he was living quite comfortably. His only concerns in life were the equipment and colleagues made available to him in his work. Why shouldn't a person be able to concentrate on his specialty and not be bothered with all the other managerial problems in life?

To be successful in our society we must reluctantly become experts, or at least quite knowledgeable, in dozens of different fields other than the one at which we are best. A person can be the best in the world at what he does (like a prizefighter, artist, craftsman, designer, inventor, scientist, teacher, lecturer, etc.) and end up an unhappy financial failure in life surrounded by unnecessary problems just because he isn't knowledgeable in the following areas or just doesn't care about them:

Real estate

Insurance

    home

    life

    automobile, RV, boat

    health

Finding a job

    negotiating a good salary with benefits

Investments

    bank accounts

checking

savings

credit unions

bonds

stocks

mutual funds

IRAs

Tax accounting

bookkeeping

constantly changing tax laws

Financing

home

cars

boats & RVs

Credit cards

Legal matters

AT&T vs. MCI vs. Sprint

and the list goes on and on!

Now we have defined the real problem, so on with the plan that will solve the majority of all these problems — hire a total personal manager. When I say total manager, I'm not talking of anything that exists today because I mean a *total* manager. I'm not talking about a person but a firm the size of TRW, Bank of America, TransAmerica, AFL/CIO, Metropolitan Ins., etc.

Let's create an illustration. I am just out of school and majored in a fairly specialized field but don't know where to find a job. I sign on with the Personal Managerial Association (PMA). From here on I am technically employed by PMA who in turn will subcontract my services to other firms. PMA will find a job for me and perform all the managerial jobs listed on the previous page. They will handle all my investments, retirement, major purchases (when I ask them to), do all my banking, compute and pay my taxes, pay all my bills, take care of my health insurance, legal matters, etc. I don't expect PMA to actually do all these things themselves but I do expect them to be knowledgeable enough to know when and where to subcontract them.

Back to the aerospace layoff experience. If firms like PMA had been in existence at that time, the firm I was working for, the employees, and the aerospace firm down the street wouldn't have had a very severe problem. Each of the aerospace firms would have had a token personnel and payroll department because they would have been dealing with PMA and a couple of similar firms. They would only make out one payroll check to each management firm like PMA instead of hundreds of thousands as they do now. When the layoff occurred, the unneeded personnel would merely have changed their commuting route the next morning and reported to the other firm for work. They wouldn't suffer any loss of seniority, vacation, retirement benefits, health benefits, etc. because PMA was their employer, not the aerospace firm.

In addition to all these benefits, the employees would enjoy the economic advantages of huge quantity discounts and group rates through PMA who would be dealing with the strength of hundreds of thousands of personnel. All these savings would more than offset the managerial fee of PMA and remove a huge load off the individual.

Economists say one of the most essential ingredients in a free enterprise system is the mobility of labor, which we have lost in today's society. Having such a huge base to work with, PMA would also know the job market throughout the whole country and probably the world. If any employee wished to move to a different state (or country), it could probably be arranged through PMA with a minimum amount of confusion.

The individual employee would not be a captive of PMA because he could discontinue the services offered by PMA at any time and perform the services himself or go with another management firm.

Large corporations should enjoy this plan because they could dispense with their personnel department, payroll department, pension programs, credit unions, health plans, life insurance plans, etc. and still have the latitude of hiring, promoting and firing their personnel by working through PMA.

The employees of smaller firms, including mom and pop stores, could enjoy the same benefits enjoyed by the employees of huge corporations now. The smaller firms would be able to expand or contract their work force without making long term commitments to their employees such as life insurance, health insurance, retirement benefits, etc. because technically they had no employees. All the personnel working there were actually employees of PMA, who handles all their benefits.

Without divine guidance such a system cannot come into being in seven days so where does it start? It should start with a single field or job market where mobility of labor is necessary due to the expansion and contraction of the business. The first examples that come to mind are the building trades in large construction jobs where jobs only last a year or two and layoffs are inevitable. Defense contractors are another example where major programs start, expand, contract, and are finished or discontinued.

During the early days of our ballistic missile programs, a plan somewhat similar to this was temporarily in effect in the Army Ballistic Missile Agency at the Redstone Arsenal. The Army knew the crash program urgency would end when the Intermediate Range Ballistic Missile program was successful and a man had been successfully placed on the moon and returned. Rather than hire huge numbers of personnel to be terminated at a later date, they contracted with the Chrysler Corp. for personnel to work for the Army. Although these were Chrysler employees, they worked at Army facilities, in Army plants, with Army tools and everything that regular Army personnel did except they wore a Chrysler badge and got a Chrysler paycheck. This allowed the Army the luxury of expanding and contracting its work force without the agony of hiring and laying off workers, and the Chrysler Corp. had a large enough labor base to absorb these shocks.

Probably the best organization to make a modest beginning to build up a Total Managerial System such as this would be what we now call a labor union, but it would be a good idea to change its name when it is changed to a total management firm. What is really needed is a firm with the combined expertise of a labor union, like the AFL/CIO, and diversified financial expertise such as TransAmerica Corp., although this would be a VERY unlikely merger. This combination of firms would be already familiar with the labor market throughout the industry and just about all phases of the financial and insurance worlds.

To create a new management firm or to convert a labor union to a management firm, there are several areas of expertise that should be approached with extreme caution. Since the managerial firm will be dealing with huge sums of money (bank accounts, insurance policies, pension plans, income taxes, mortgages, etc.) they should be careful to avoid hiring any of the ex-managers that drove some of the Savings and Loan firms into bankruptcy (no unsecured loans to third world countries).

This idea has been lying around in my head for over thirty years and its time has come. There definitely is a need for total management firms, and their evolvement is a certainty in the not too distant future, IN MY OPINION, and that's what this book is all about.

In a democratic government there are literally thousands of issues to be studied, approved or disapproved — Far too many and varied for the average citizen to be concerned, so we give our power of attorney to somebody who shares our views and who will handle these governmental political matters full time. I think that makes us a Republic. The Total Manager will perform the same type of function for us in our personal life. Make sense?

Chapter 20

MINIMUM WAGES

We have a minimum wage law in the United States which is absolutely contrary to all principles of a free enterprise economy. This has come about by a bunch of sob sister politicians making it appear that they are the saviors of our economy, helping the poor and doing great humanitarian things. Nothing could be further from the truth and here is the rationale for these bold statements.

Let us use a large corporation as an example and further assume that it has 10 pay grades in its wage structure. In this illustration the present minimum wage scale is $3.00 per hour. After the politicians have made many speeches to raise their popularity with the lowest wage earners, they point out that people making a mere $3.00 per hour are unable to live comfortably. Then they initiate a discussion as to whether there should be a sixty cent per hour or a seventy-five cent per hour increase in the minimum wage. Those who enter into the debate of sixty cents versus seventy-five cents have unwittingly conceded that a legal minimum wage law is OK. Note how carefully they gloss over the real issue which is — should there be a minimum wage or not?

It is also part of the political strategy to make anyone opposing the raising of the minimum wage appear cold-hearted, ruthless and uncaring. They have made it political suicide to talk against a minimum wage law. After the political dust has settled, it is finally decided that the sixty cent per hour increase would be appropriate. Let us further assume for the sake of this illustration that this increase only applies to Plant A of the corporation and not to Plant B of the same corporation that produces the identical product. The bill is passed, and the hero politicians smugly pat themselves on the back, knowing they have bought many votes at the next election from the mass of lowest wage earners who aren't aware that their jobs and our economy have been further sabotaged. There are two ways of looking at this raise. It is either $.60 (across the board) or, more realistically, it is a 20% increase. Using purely hypothetical numbers, we can illustrate what happens when our sob sister politicians raise the minimum wage scale in the following chart:

WAGE SCALE	CURRENT WAGES	$.60 RAISE	20% RAISE
#1 (Minimum Wage)	$3.00	$3.60	$3.60
#2	$4.00	$4.60	$4.80
#3	$5.00	$5.60	$6.00
#4	$6.00	$6.60	$7.20
#5	$7.00	$7.60	$8.40
#6	$8.00	$8.60	$9.60

#7	$9.00	$9.60	$10.80
#8	$10.00	$10.60	$12.00
#9	$11.00	$11.60	$13.20
#10	$12.00	$12.60	$14.40

Raising the minimum wage from $3.00 to $3.60 has had an almost immediate cascading effect throughout Plant A of the corporation all the way up the wage scale ladder. Any politician who denies this and says that those who work in pay grades 2 through 10 will continue to work at their old wages rates, which were unaffected by the new minimum wage law, flunked both arithmetic and psychology in school, and if you believe their argument please call me as I have two bridges and one tunnel I'd like to sell you.

In the above illustration, since it is mine, I set the rules. Plant B of the corporation happens to be in a foreign country that has a lower cost of living and has no minimum wage scale and workers are most pleased to work for the equivalent of about $1.00 U.S. per hour. The natural conclusion is that the United States has further damaged its competitive position in the world market, and some of the workers in Plant A of the corporation are wondering where their jobs went while Plant B is hiring more workers and celebrating.

If you are old enough, you may recall when the U.S. produced sewing machines, bicycles, televisions, radios, motorcycles, and literally hundreds of other items, including almost all of the world's automobiles, which we no longer produce. When I was young, the only foreign automobiles in the annual automobile show were the Citroen, the English Swallow and, I think, the MG. The most luxurious and expensive car in the show was the 12-cylinder Packard Seven Passenger Limousine which sold for $9,300. A foreign car on the street here in the U.S. was so rare it would draw a huge crowd of curiosity seekers. I wonder if this equates to our minimum wage law some way?

In science we learned that the whole is equal to the sum of its parts and labor is definitely a part of the cost of any finished product. If you want to have some sadistic fun, ask your politician to refute this argument. You will hear political side-stepping like you've never heard before.

If for some reason I have not convinced you of my logic, try a little logic of your own. If some is good, then more is better, or is the current philosophy that a little bit of damage is OK? Why a $3.00 per hour minimum wage? Let's make it $6.00 per hour, $10.00 per hour or even $100.00 per hour. If the minimum wage was $100.00 per hour, how much would a Big Mac cost us and would there be any American cars produced and sold?

A long time ago when the minimum wage law was first passed, we thought only in terms of our U.S. economy, but this is no longer the situation. The U.S. economy is a thing of the past, and we must learn to think in terms of the world economy thanks to greatly improved transportation, education and communications. Our competitors are at our door rather than worlds away.

The obvious remedy is to eliminate the minimum wage law, but no politician in his right mind would ever crusade such a politically suicidal program. The next best approach would be to link the minimum wage to the balance (or imbalance) of trade or, better yet, just leave it alone and *never* touch it again. Eventually, as the production costs in the rest of the world catch up to us, our minimum wage law will become totally ineffective, and that's the way it should be.

Permission is hereby granted to anyone who wishes to reproduce this argument to be sent to their congressman. SEE APPENDIX B.

Chapter 21

THE SOLUTION

"The only thing necessary for the triumph of evil is for good men to do nothing." — Edmund Burke (1729-1797)

Tolerance is usually an admirable trait, but continued tolerance of an undesirable situation tends to give it an air of acceptability. Tolerance can also be an excuse for procrastination and total inactivity. How long have we complained about continued deficit spending, the injustices and over complexity of the income tax code, the illegal alien situation, narcotics, etc. — and yet we continue to accept them as a way of life?

If you got this far in the book, you are probably convinced that a lot of things in this world need fixing even if you don't agree with any of my suggested solutions. Well, what are YOU going to do about all this? Remember there is no "they" in this democracy. *"WE ARE THEY."* I couldn't think of anything else to do about these things, so I wrote this book hoping a great many people with intellect and drive will get off their complacency and straighten out this unnecessarily complicated world by applying logic and an abundance of SIMPLICITY. Go for it. Let's see some action!

Probably the majority of our pressing problems are closely associated with Congress so this should be our number one pressure point for stimulation for resolutions. If Congress refuses to act on these problems, then we must seriously consider a new congress. Every politician should be required to write a book such as this one before running for an elective office so we will know his views in some detail on many subjects. Being a literary genius isn't required — I have proven that. His book would give us a yardstick by which to measure his performance while in office. It should also eliminate many surprises. Each of his objectives should have a timetable connected to it so we can differentiate a lackluster performance from an enthusiastic charge. Unfortunately, the solution to many of these problems requires that Congress straighten out itself and this is highly unlikely without an overwhelming amount of stimulation. Here is where you come in. We lack the necessary tool, a national referendum, because it is not provided in the constitution to enable us to override Congress. Congress doesn't want a national referendum. We need this necessary tool to override Congress to get the necessary tool to override Congress. This is called circular thinking or "Catch 22." What would you say the chances are of this happening? Confusing isn't it. If Congress won't straighten out itself it is up to us to straighten them out.

There comes a time in the life of an automobile where a decision must be made as to whether to repair the old car or replace it with a new one. This holds true for congressmen also. First let's take a shot at repairing the old ones. Write your congressman, whether you voted for him or not, he is your congressman. To assist you in writing your first letter, it is suggested you reread the sample letter on page 80.

CAUTION — One of our biggest mistakes in this world is confusing change and progress. We got into this mess due to many changes made without proper thought. When a mistake is made, don't let our stubborn pride force us to perpetuate the mistake when our better judgment tells us differently. After Sputnik was launched, our IGY (International Geophysical Year) space program was a string of failures. Dutch Kindleberger, CEO of North American Aviation, was consulted by a congressional committee on how to salvage our nation's ailing space effort. Dutch told them, "The best way *not* to untangle a ball of yarn was to wrap more yarn around it," and the very next day Congress ignored his advise and created another governmental agency. Either they listened with closed ears or they only heard what they wanted to hear.

Stimulating Congress into action is too big a job for any one person, so let's recruit all the help we can get. Here are some of the targets for you to shoot at.

– Write lots and lots of letters to politicians, newspapers, magazines, friends, etc. We must be careful dealing with the news media for they love a mess, because without it they wouldn't have much to write about. Don't worry very much about this being a problem, because it is highly unlikely that this world will ever run so smoothly that the news media will have nothing to write about. They are also the self-appointed leaders of our society, and if things were as simple as they ought to be, their influence would diminish drastically. Here's another worry you can forget.

– Radio call-in programs — Careful, they don't like cuckoos and it's easy to sound like one if you get too far outside the mainstream of complacency and tolerance where most of us dwell. Like all of us, talk show hosts have mood swings also. If they are in an argumentative mood, they welcome the opposition so they cut them up into small pieces. On the other hand if they're in an "eh" mood, they tend to cut off the opposition without much argument and deny them much airtime that day. They usually like people who agree with them, so at least appear that way if possible to achieve a modest amount of airtime.

– It's OK to complain about the way things are now and have an opinion that is far from the main stream of sheep voters (voters who follow the leader so they won't have to think for themselves) provided you have an alternative plan or solution to the problem and don't use the policeman's choke hold to impose your ideas on society. There are two things to be said for being a sheep voter. The obvious is that you are not required to think for yourself, and the other advantage is you are among the majority so you can let others defend their position which happens to coincide with yours.

Appendix A is my pressure point target list for my locality, presented here as a model for your homework assignment, which is to write an Appendix A for your locality, and then let's see how much good we can do. We have a very fine country and government, but all this didn't come about through the efforts of "rugged complacentists" with a severe case of "rockingchairitis."

Life is somewhat like sports. There are active and dedicated participants, lackluster participants, officials, fans (fanatics), mere observers (who really don't know or care what is going on and are only there because a friend dragged them there), and then there are those who don't even go to the game and even some who think the game should be outlawed. Which is your classification? The whole idea of this book is to encourage you to upgrade your classification and get more involved.

Now that you are inspired and ready to go forth into the world to do some good you must be forewarned that there are some unfriendly groups to be reckoned with out there. Here are a few groups to look out for.

CFSC   Change for the Sake of Change — these people are quick draw artists that shoot from the hip and then look to see what they've done.

SQS   Status Quo Syndrome — if it was good enough for my pappy it's good enough for me. If it involves change — forget it!

IDK   I Don't Know — who cares, I can't do anything about it. This is a high priority target for you to work on with your verbal needles.

NIMBY   Not In My Back Yard — Sure we want a strong Navy but don't put the Battleship Missouri in my San Francisco Bay. Yeah, we need more prisons but not here.

DUMAC   Don't Upset My Apple Cart — it's a good idea to change the IRS codes by eliminating those loopholes but don't touch my deductions. This group is headed by members of Lobbyists

International* and includes the majority of our congressmen. Close some military bases and save some money, but don't touch my state.

A quotable quote from the office walls of a friend of mine.

"There is no limit to the amount of good one can do — if he doesn't care who gets the credit." *Gene Van Dask*

Lobbyists International exists only in my imagination.

Appendix A

ACTION LIST

YOUR OPINION IS SOMEWHAT WORTHLESS UNLESS YOU MAKE IT KNOWN IN THE RIGHT PLACES. In case you've missed it, this is the whole theme of this book.

The solution to a great many of our problems lies in straightening out our government, so let me introduce you to some people who heretofore have probably been strangers to the majority of us and we have remained a stranger to them. Make up your own target list and use it frequently. The following list is your starter kit for you to expand upon. Your telephone directory will be your best friend in this regard.

GOVERNMENT TARGETS

Federal

U.S. Senator Pete Wilson
Senate Office Bldg.
Washington D. C. 20510

U.S. Senator Alan Cranston
Senate Office Bldg.
Washington D. C. 20510

U.S. Congressman
Geo. Miller III
2228 Rayburn Bldg.
Washington, D. C. 20515
(202) 225-2095

House Ways & Means
Committee
Congressman
Dan Rostenkowski
Chairman
House of Representatives
Washington D C, 20515

U.S. Congressman - 4th Dist.
Vic Fazio
2525 Natomas Park Dr.
Sacramento, Ca.
(916) 978-4381

U.S. Congressman - 3rd Dist.
Robert T. Mantusi
650 Capitol Mall
Sacramento, Ca.
(916) 551-2846

U.S. Congressman - 14th Dist.
Norman D. Shumway
1159 W. Robinhood
Stockton, Ca. (209) 957-7773

STATE TARGETS

Senator Dan Boatwright
State Capitol Bldg.
Sacramento, Ca. 95814
or
420 w. Third Street
Antioch, Ca. 94509

Assemblyman Robert Campbell
State Office Bldg.
Sacramento, Ca. 95814

2010 Railroad Avenue
Pittsburg, Ca. 94565

Assemblyman Phil Isenberg
State Capitol Bldg.
Sacramento, Ca. 95814

Assemblyman Bill Baker
1243 Alpine Road
Walnut Creek, Ca.

Contra Costa County
Supervisor Tom Torlakson
300 E. Leland Road
Suite 100
Pittsburg, Ca. 94565

NEWSPAPERS (RECRUITING OFFICES)

Here is where we get support to promote our ideas

Local
Letters to the Editor
Brentwood News
654 3rd Street
Brentwood, Ca. 94513
(415) 634-2125

San Francisco Chronicle
901 Mission Street
San Francisco, Ca. 94103

Daily Ledger - Post Dispatch
1650 Cavallo Road
Antioch, Ca. 94509
(415) 757 2525

Oakland Tribune
(no letters to the editor)

Sacramento Bee
2100 Q Street
Sacramento, Ca.
(916) 321-1001 Editorial

Sacramento Union
301 Capitol Mall
Sacramento, Ca.
(916) 442-7811

Stockton Record
Speaking Out
P. O. Box 900
Stockton, Ca. 95201

Placer Herald
5903 Sunset Blvd.
Rocklin, Ca. 95677
(916) 624-9713

National
Time, Inc.
Time & Life Bldg.
Rockefeller Center
New York, N. Y. 10020
FAX (212) 522-0907

U S News & World Report
2400 N Street NW
Washington, D.C. 20037-1196
(202) 955-2000

NEWSWEEK
444 Madison Ave.
New York, N.Y. 10022
New York, N Y 10020-1393

Sports Illustrated
Time & Life Bldg.
Rockefeller Center

Wall Street Journal
200 Liberty Street
New York, N Y 10281

SOURCE MATERIALS

Rocklin Public Library
5460 5th Street
Rocklin, Ca. 95677
(916) 624-3133

Brentwood Public Library
(415) 634-4101

Republican Headquarters

Democratic Headquarters

U. S. Government Printing Office
Washington, D. C.

RADIO STATION CALL-IN PROGRAMS

My Local Radio Stations
KGO
Jim Eason (Talk Show Hosts)
Ron Owens
900 Front Street
Oakland, Ca. 94111
(415) 938-TALK

Make up your own target list for your area so it will be handy when you need it. Once you have made up your list you will have no excuse for not using it. Almost all this information came directly from the telephone directory. Look under Federal Government in the front of your directory. *Make your opinions known* (particularly if they happen to agree with mine).

.

THE END

(hopefully, it's your beginning)

Appendix B

SPREAD THE WORD OFFER

GIVE AN INSPIRATIONAL WAKE UP CALL
TO SOMEONE

If you wish to rattle someone's cage by having a copy of this book or only a chapter of it sent to a friend, enemy, politician, newspaper, magazine, commentator, school, college, etc. along with your comments, just send the following to:

OPINIONS

Post Office Box Number 1591

Rocklin, Calif. 95677

1. Your letter of transmittal addressed to the desired recipient

2. Your check

each book - $6.95* plus $1.95 (postage, sales tax & handling)

each chapter - $1.50* plus $.95 (postage sales tax & handling)

- write for quantity discounts -

Anonymous is acceptable - I'll keep your secret! If your addressee is a national politician, give me the office he or she holds and I'll do the rest for you.

I sincerely hope you have enjoyed this book and are now inspired to make YOUR opinions known where they will do the most good. It is a very satisfying feeling. I would enjoy your comments also.

* *Prices subject to change.*

Appendix C

GROUP YOUR TARGETS BY CATEGORY

United States Congress
    Senators
    Representatives
    Committees

Cabinet Members

National News Media

Magazines

Special Groups:
    Democratic Party Headquarters
    Republican Party Headquarters
    League of Women Voters
    Republican Women's Club
    Libertarian Party Headquarters

State Legislatures
    Senators
    Representatives
    Committees

Department Heads

Local News Media

Radio Stations

When writing a letter, remember "If one is good, then two (or more) is better" and copies are cheap. Use the shotgun approach and hit them all

Name: _____

Address _____

_____

Attn: _____

Name: _____

Address _____

_____

Attn: _____

Name: _____

Address _____

_____

Attn: _____

Name: _____

Address _____

_____

Attn: _____

Name: _____

Address _____

_____

Attn: _____

Name: _____

Address _____

_____

Attn: _____

Name: _____
Address _____
_____
Attn: _____

Name: _____
Address _____
_____
Attn: _____

Name: _____
Address _____
_____
Attn: _____

Name: _____
Address _____
_____
Attn: _____

Name: _____
Address _____
_____
Attn: _____

Name: _____
Address _____
_____
Attn: _____

EVERYBODY'S ENTITLED TO MY OPINION

Name: _____
Address _____
_____
Attn: _____

Name: _____
Address _____
_____
Attn: _____

Name: _____
Address _____
_____
Attn: _____

Name: _____
Address _____
_____
Attn: _____

Name: _____
Address _____
_____
Attn: _____

Name: _____
Address _____
_____
Attn: _____